Francesca Alexander

Christ's Folk in the Apennine

Francesca Alexander

Christ's Folk in the Apennine

ISBN/EAN: 9783337165505

Printed in Europe, USA, Canada, Australia, Japan

Cover: Foto ©ninafisch / pixelio.de

More available books at **www.hansebooks.com**

Prof. John Ruskin, 1866. *See page* 32.

BY
FRANCESCA ALEXANDER.

EDITED BY
JOHN RUSKIN, D.C.L.,
Honorary Student of Christ Church, and Honorary Fellow of Corpus Christi College, Oxford.

I.
THE PEACE OF POLISSENA.

GEORGE ALLEN,
SUNNYSIDE, ORPINGTON, KENT.
1887

Price One Shilling.

CHRIST'S FOLK.

CHRIST'S FOLK

IN THE APENNINE.

REMINISCENCES
OF HER FRIENDS
AMONG THE TUSCAN PEASANTRY.

BY
FRANCESCA ALEXANDER.

EDITED BY
JOHN RUSKIN, D.C.L.,
Honorary Student of Christ Church, and Honorary Fellow of Corpus Christi College, Oxford.

GEORGE ALLEN,
SUNNYSIDE, ORPINGTON, KENT.
1887.

Printed by Hazell, Watson, & Viney, Ld., London and Aylesbury.

CHRIST'S FOLK

IN THE APENNINE.

REMINISCENCES
OF HER FRIENDS
AMONG THE TUSCAN PEASANTRY.

BY

FRANCESCA ALEXANDER.

EDITED BY

JOHN RUSKIN, D.C.L.,

Honorary Student of Christ Church, and Honorary Fellow of Corpus Christi College, Oxford.

I.

THE PEACE OF POLISSENA.

GEORGE ALLEN,
SUNNYSIDE, ORPINGTON, KENT.
1887.

Printed by Hazell, Watson, & Viney, Ld., London and Aylesbury.

PREFACE.

SINCE first I received from Miss Alexander the trusts involved in the editorship of the " Story of Ida" and " Songs of Tuscany," she has been in the habit of writing to me little sketches or stories of her peasant friends, as they chance to visit her, either, as it often happens, for the simple pleasure of talking to her, or silently watching her at her work,—or, as it still oftener happens, when they seek her counsel in their troubles, or her sympathy in their good fortune. Her door is never closed to them ; the drawing in progress advances under her hand with the same tranquillity through the children's babble and the mother's boast; and time is never wanting if they need her attentive care, or active help. Her letters usually contain at least a page or two of chat about the visitors who have been claiming her immediate notice, or some reminiscence of former passages between them, which the affectionate historian, finding me hardly less interested in her favourites than she was herself, and interested in the way she wished, gradually completed and developed, until now I find under my hand a series of word-portraits, finished as tenderly as her drawings, and of even higher value in their accuracy of penetration, for the written sketches contain little gleams of gentle satire which never occur in the drawings. And it seems to me that the best Christmas work I can do this year, (my own fields of occupation being also in great measure closed to me by the severe warning of recent illness and the languor it has left,) will be to gather out of this treasure of letters what part might, with the writer's permission, and without pain to any of her loved friends, be laid before those of the English public who have either seen enough of the Italian peasantry to recognise the truth of these *ritratti*, or have respect enough for the faith of the incorrupt Catholic Church to admit the sincerity, and rejoice in the virtue, of a people still living as in the presence of Christ, and under the instant teaching of His saints and apostles. I shall change no word in the familiar language of the letters, nor attempt any other arrangement than that of merely collating the passages referring at intervals to the same person, nor even this with any strictness. For it is one of the pleasantest features in the tenor of these annals to have our friends coming to see us again at their different ages, and in their added dignities of possession or position.

The story with which I begin is, however, a little different from the others, having been written for me by Francesca in consequence of my complaint that the "Story of Ida" was too sad, and conceded too much to the modern feeling of the British public that people who are quite good have nothing to do but to die. The story of Polissena may perhaps never reach the same place in the reader's heart; but it is in the depth of it far more bravely and widely exemplary.

BRANTWOOD,
30th November, 1886.

CONTENTS.

		PAGE
I. THE PEACE OF POLISSENA	. .	1
II. "PENSATEVI VOI!" . .	.	47
III. THE MOTHER OF THE ORPHANS	. .	71
IV. THE NUN'S SCHOOL IN FLORENCE—		

I. THE NUN'S SCHOOL IN FLORENCE	. .	127
II. POLISSENA "IN VENA" . . .	.	138
III. FRANCESCA'S BEE	.	140
IV. ENRICHETTA'S NIGHTINGALES .	.	143
V. ROSITA AND ANGELINA . .	.	144
VI. INTO GOOD HANDS	.	151
VII. RIVALTA	.	156
VIII. ST. MARK STILL PREACHES .	.	166
IX. ENRICHETTA'S CHARITY . .	.	171

V. "ADDIO, CARA!"—

I. KINDNESS OF THE WILD WEST .	.	177
II. ROSSINI'S RETURN TO FLORENCE	.	180
III. THE LOVE OF THE DUOMO .	.	184
IV. THE LOCANDA AT BASSANO .	.	188
V. THE PATRIARCH OF VENICE .	.	195
VI. THE ARMENIAN IDA . . .	.	201
VII. IN THE DARK VALLEY . .	.	207
VIII. "ADDIO, CARA!" . . .	.	212

VI. LIETI ANDIAMO—

		PAGE
I. THE KNITTING FOR CESIRA	. . .	221
II. THE STORY OF THE SAVINGS BANK	. .	226
III. ROSITA, AND GIACOMO BONI	. . .	231
IV. THE STORY OF SANTA ROSA	. . .	238
V. THE DOGE'S DAUGHTER	. . .	243
VI. HOW ST. PETER LOST HIS TEMPER	. .	246
VII. THE STORY OF THE BISHOP OF VERONA	.	251
VIII. LIETI ANDIAMO	. . . .	256

THE PEACE OF POLISSENA.

SEVERAL years ago—I should think about twelve—I used to see a party of three young people, strangers at Abetone, working in the woods, and they attracted my attention, because one of them was a girl who shared in all the boys' work, and seemed to take the general direction of whatever was done.

They used to lodge at night in the house of old Margherita of the Cima, and her blind son Fortunato; and as I was in the habit, while Margherita lived, of going often to see her and listen to her stories, I soon made acquaintance with the young strangers.

The girl, Polissena, was then apparently about fourteen or fifteen years old, and she looked poor, and not very strong, and she was not in the least pretty, only she had a pretty smile, and her manners were gentle and modest. The two boys, one a little older and the other a little younger than herself, were her brothers; their father had lately died, and Polissena, being the energetic one of the family, had quite naturally stepped into his place as head.

What I have now to tell about her became known to me little by little, in the course of all the years that have passed since; and though her life is one of few events, I think it is worth writing down, if only for the reason that she seems to me, taking her whole life together, to be the happiest person whom I ever knew.

This morning I have had a visit from her,

and have been asking her many questions about herself; and her answers to them, and what I have heard of her from others, will enable me to tell the story connectedly. One question I could not ask her: I know that away somewhere near the beginning of Polissena's life there was some terrible tragedy; but I do not rightly know what it was.

The neighbours call her "La Bruciata," and she bears the mark of some frightful accident. One of her hands has been so injured by the fire as to have hardly the shape of a hand at all, so that she has been cut off from every kind of "woman's work;" she cannot sew, nor knit, nor spin; nobody would take her for a servant, nobody will ever marry her. And I have known some, less afflicted than she, who have lived on charity, or been burdens on their families

But she began, when a very little girl, to share her brothers' work; and used to go with them into the woods to collect weeds for the horses, or wood for the house.

Her father went *trapelo*, as they say here: that is, he lived at Ponte a Cutigliano, just at the foot of the steep ascent to L'Abetone, and he kept one or two large strong horses, which could be fastened to any wagon or carriage, in front of whatever horses there might be already, and would help drag it to the highest part of the road; the owner walking along beside them all the way.

When Polissena's father died, *she* used to go *trapelo*, taking turns with her elder brother; the great, strong horses would obey her voice perfectly.

As she said to me this morning, when I asked her how the horses all came to be so obedient:

"My brothers and I like our horses, and take good care of them, and never beat them; and the horses know, and will listen to everything we say. Some of the barocciai here beat and kick their horses; I cannot bear to see them; and the horses will not let them come near them if they can help it: horses know, just the same as Christians, when people are good to them."

She used to feed and take care of the horses, and at other times would go and load wood with the men; indeed, I had to wait for several days before I could have a visit from her, because she and her brother had an engagement loading beans. She has passed her life doing men's work of the roughest sort, and must, I should think, be often in the roughest sort of company; and I should have supposed that if anything would take all the womanliness out of a woman, it would be such a life as that.

But now I come to just what I wanted to say about Polissena, and what some one else will have to explain, for I cannot: her strange rough life has neither injured her, nor made her unhappy. She is singularly gentle and refined in manner, and I should think in character; never feels herself degraded by her work or her surroundings, or envies other women who are, or seem to be, less unfortunate;—indeed, she would be very much surprised if she should hear that any-one considered her unfortunate at all.

People call her "piuttosto bellina," yet there is not a good feature in her face, and sun and wind have made her complexion more like that of a sailor than a woman: there is really nothing good-looking about her, excepting a graceful though rather meagre little figure, and white regular teeth; she has a pinched, poverty-stricken face, as of one who has suffered in childhood. And yet people like to look at her! She does look good, and kind, and truthful, and I can see that she grows better-looking with time, as very good people usually do, and there is a certain placid happiness in her face, which makes it very pleasant to look at, in spite of its plainness. She has the softest, sweetest voice that ever was given to a woman, and much grace of manner. This grace, indeed, is common to a great many of the mountain women, but Polissena has something more, in her real kindness of heart, and interest in all those about her. She is not a great talker, being too busy for gossip, but when I do have a chance to talk with her, she always says something that I like to remember. If she asks a favour of any one, she always asks it " Per amor mio!" and such an appeal, made in the full confidence that everybody loves her, just as she loves everybody, seldom fails.

I should have supposed that her life would have been the harder to her for the very reason that she is so very "womanly" in taste and character, so fond of everything pretty and peaceful. But the womanly side of her nature finds an outlet in her love of flowers. In the steep hill-side garden behind her house, where she raises beans and potatoes for the family, and does more work, it seems to me sometimes, with her one available hand, than any two men with a good pair of hands each, Polissena has her flower garden,—quite an "institution" in that part of the country,—where she raises a great variety of really beautiful flowers. I ought to know something about it; for every now and then some passer-by leaves a basket at our door, and when I open it I know in a minute who sent it. First a layer of chestnut leaves, to keep out the sun, and under that a pile of flowers, laid carefully, so as not to hurt each other; splendid roses and carnations, and other choice flowers, and with them some of the more beautiful of the wild flowers that grow about Cutigliano; and under these the basket half full of beans, or cherries, or new potatoes, as the case may be, with always a little bunch of sweet herbs for the soup;—really a valuable present in this place, where *nothing* is to be bought.

I asked her if the men among whom she was obliged to work were never uncivil or profane. She said that they had never been uncivil to *her*; that they would not be so to any girl who was quiet and minded her own business; but she acknowledged that they were often profane. "I wonder," she said, "how they can speak bad words of the Almighty, as they do, and then, as soon as they are in any trouble, be asking Him to help them. But of course they have no one else to go to. Who else *can* help us? It is just as if I should abuse you and call you names, and then when I wanted something, come and ask you to give it to me. I am sure you would not give me anything. God does help the people who abuse Him, because He is so good; but I think that He must like better to help the people that love Him." I said to her, "You seem to love Him." She answered, "Oh, yes, of course I love Him, because He has been so good to *me*" (with a little emphasis on the "me," as if she hardly supposed He could be quite so good to other people). "He gives me such good health, and He almost always gives me what I want if I ask Him, and He has helped me so often when I was in trouble!" I asked her if she never felt it hard to have to do such heavy work. She smiled, and said, "Oh, but it is such a pleasure to work when one has good health. I do not think there is anything else so pleasant as working! My sister—do you not know her? She is larger than I, and a great deal prettier, but she is not so strong, and she cannot do the sort of hard work that I can: she stays at home and helps my mother, or she goes to pick berries at the Cerchietto. But if she should have to go for berries to the Sassi Scritti, as I have to, sometimes, she would not be able to bear it. She thought of going to service at Pistoia, but we cannot bear to part with her, and really there is no need of it, for we have everything quite comfortable at home, and enough for all our wants."

I asked her what she meant by the Sassi Scritti, and she gave me quite an interesting account of them, which I will give as nearly as possible in her own words.

"Up over Pian degli Ontani there is a mountain, very hard even for me to climb, that they call Sassi Scritti, because the rocks up at the top of the mountain have words cut in them. I cannot read them, none of our people can. It is a different sort of writing from that which we know, but very beautiful to look at; and they say that the words were cut there by people who lived a very long time ago, nobody knows how long.

"I go there sometimes for blueberries, in the season when the dealers come up from Pistoia, and other places on the plain, to buy them ; you know that they buy blueberries to make wine. One day I had gone there with a large party of people ; we had climbed a great way, and picked a great many berries, when there came up a great storm, but really a terrible storm, with thunder and lightning, and a deluge of rain ; so that we had to leave our berries and only think of saving ourselves. We were running toward some trees, thinking to take refuge under them ; but there was an old man among us, a very good old man, and we generally did everything that he said ; and he told us that we must not go under the trees, because the lightning would strike there, if it did anywhere ; but that he would take us to a safe place. Then we climbed a little more, and he brought us to a place where the great rocks were piled together, and made a sort of cave, and he told us to go in. I was frightened at first—it was a beautiful place, but strange and fearful-looking, and I thought perhaps the lightning would come in after us; but he said there was no danger.

"So we waited there a long time, with the storm going on outside, and I looked at the rocks about us; they were all written with those strange words that none of us could read. But you cannot think how beautiful it all was! And late in the day, after the storm had cleared, the old man said:

"'We have lost our day's work; but if you like to come with me I will show you something worth seeing!'

"Then he made us climb just a little farther, and brought us to the crest of the mountain, and then he *did* show us something beautiful! Only it was all so strange! I never saw anything like it in my life!

The land was spread out flat like water—I thought at first it *was* water. And far away, on this level land, I saw something white, as if a strip of white cloth had been laid on the ground; and the old man told us that was Florence!"

I asked Polissena to tell me a little about her family. She said that her eldest brother, whom I remembered having seen years ago, had lost his life in Sardegna.

"He went several years ago to Sardegna," she said, "and he had great fortune there. He entered the service of a very rich lady, who employed a great many workmen; and she liked my brother very much, and set him over the other workmen, and used to send him to pay them at the end of the week. And people knew that he had the money to pay the workmen, and they formed a plan to rob him. One pay-day they lay in wait for him at a lonely part of the road which he had to pass, and they fired upon him as he went by upon his horse, and so he died. You can imagine what a grief this was to all of us, to have him die so far from us, and in such a way! My poor brother—he was so good! We had not seen him for two years, but all the money that he earned he used to send home to my mother. The people who killed him did not gain anything by it after all, for he had sent the money that day for the workmen by another hand."

By this time, seeing that her eyes were full of tears, I tried to lead her to speak of her mother and of her two younger brothers. I told her that it must be a great comfort to her mother to have a daughter who would work for her, and take care of her as she did.

"Oh," she said quickly, as if she did not like the idea of her mother being under obligation to her. "But my mother is so good! She is so good to me, and you cannot think how happy we are together!"

Her second brother, who has some employment out of the house, is married, and lives at Pian degli Ontani; Polissena is a little anxious about him and his young wife. She says: "I hope the good Lord will take care of them, and guide all their affairs for the best, but I never can see how they are going to live. I love my sister-in-law; really I love her in my heart, but I cannot understand her."

I asked her what it was that she found difficult of comprehension in the character of her brother's wife. She thought a little, for she is not used to putting her thoughts into words, then she said:

"She is poor, and I rather think she does not like to be poor; and she wants to behave as if she were rich: and you know if God has made us poor we *must* live like poor people. She does not like to work: I think she makes a mistake, I find work such a great pleasure, but of course people cannot all feel alike."

And now I will end this story, which is growing a great deal too long, by telling what she told me about an illness which this brother had, and his wonderful recovery, a year or so before his marriage.

"My brother, the one who works for a master, had been travelling a long way with the horses, and he was very warm and tired. When night came on he lay down and slept under the open sky, on the damp ground; it was a cold night, and he took an illness which almost brought him to his grave. The doctor gave him over, the priest came and gave him the last sacraments, and we were expecting him to die every hour, when it pleased the Lord to give him back to us in a very wonderful way. He was lying insensible, as we thought, breathing very slowly, and he looked like one already dead. The evening had come, and they all said he would not see the morning; the priest was waiting to help him with his prayers at the last moment, and a neighbour had come to stay with him through the night, for my mother could not stay in the room. I went in to look once more at my poor brother, and the priest was just telling me that it was all as good as over, he would never revive again; when, as I bent over his face, he opened his eyes, and I saw that he knew me. And he said, in a voice so faint that I could hardly hear it, 'Stay with me.' Then his eyes closed again, and I thought, 'I shall die too.' But I would not leave him, and I sat down by his side. I sat there a great while! After a long time the priest and the neighbour went away for a while (they used to go out into the air sometimes for fear of contagion), and I was left alone with my brother. While I was alone with him his breathing changed; he began to draw long breaths with pauses between, as if they were the very last. And I—I suppose I was out of my head. I did not rightly know what I was doing, but it was that feeling that I must do something. I took up a bottle of vinegar that was on the table, and bathed his forehead with it. As soon as I had done so, the priest and the other man came back again. They came to look at him, and they began to say, 'His forehead is wet!' Then I told what I had done, and they were very angry with me: the priest scolded me well! But my brother opened his eyes, and he said, 'Polissena, what have you done to me, that you have brought me back to the world?' Afterwards he said, 'Did you see me when I made you a sign to pray for me?' But the end of it all was, that in a few days from that time he was well and about again!"

I asked Polissena if she had understood her brother's sign, and if she had been praying for him. She blushed a little, and dropped her voice, as she said, "When I was alone with him I knelt down by the bed, and said the 'Santo Verbo' three times over. That is a prayer that obtains a great many good answers, they say it hardly ever fails."

I asked her to teach me the Santo Verbo; and she then recited to me, with much devotion, a string of doggerel rhymes, alluding to several sacred events, but without a word of anything that could be called prayer, from beginning to end. "But you must say it *three times*, you know," she said, as she came to the end. I thought that I might have said it thirty without its doing me any good.

So I asked her if that was *all* she said, "because," said I, "you do not ask for anything with that prayer." She answered, "I say to the Lord, 'Do please give me what I need so much, *per amor mio!*' Of course He knows all about it, so there is no need of saying more than that."

About that time Polissena thought she must go home, where she was wanted to put some sticks to the beans; but as she turned around at the door to take leave of me, with her peculiar modest grace, I found that I had quite come round to the neighbours' opinion that she was "piuttosto bellina," myself.

I think, although I tried hard to give a faithful likeness, that the picture gives no idea of what is best in her face; her features are like what I have drawn, but her face, when she speaks, lights into great brilliancy. While drawing her, I learned several things more about her. To my surprise, I find that she knows how to read very well, though she has never been to school: this is the account which she gave me of her education:

"When I was a little child I used to be a good deal in the house of some neighbours, who were quite rich people. The father wished very much that his daughter, who was a very pretty girl, and much older than I, should learn to read, and he paid a master to come to the house and teach her. But she would never attend to her lessons, and used to try her master's patience until he hardly knew what to do. The truth is, she was in love; and her lover (whom she afterwards married) was always coming in to talk with her, and so she did not care about the reading. The master used to say: 'What a pity you will not learn, when your poor father pays so much to have you taught!' But she would not mind what he said, and so, as he had nothing to do, he used to say to me, 'Little girl, don't *you* want to learn?' I was only too well pleased, and he taught me to read very well."

I asked her what books she had, and she said, "One or two books of prayers, and the 'Via del Paradiso.'"

I do not think she needs that last book

very much; it seems to me that she knows the "way to heaven" already, and is walking in it straiter than most of us do. Her faith is so great, and her conscience so clear, that she has no fear for this world or the next.

She says: "God has given us death, but He has given us heaven too!" After thinking a little, she added: "He wants us to deserve it; but then, there are so many to pray for us. You know up in heaven there are so many angels! And all the people who do no harm, and never speak evil of their neighbours, the angels pray for them. Besides, we can pray for ourselves, and ask God to give us what we want in the other world, just as we do when we want anything here, and He will be *sure* to give it to us! Up in heaven, they say, we shall have always music and singing; I suppose they will have all *good* songs, not like a great many that one hears about the country here; perhaps the music will sound something like the church bells; they say those are the Lord's voice!"

I asked her about her brother who married the incomprehensible young lady who does not like to work.

She said, "They are doing very well; my brother likes work well enough for both of them; he is in Sardegna now; he has not come home this summer, and he sends all his money to his wife at Pian degli Ontani."

(Really I think this may be called an unselfish attachment—to live all the year round in Sardegna, at the risk of Maremma fever, and never see the object of his affections, but content himself with the happiness of working to maintain her in idleness!)

I wanted to buy some potatoes of Polissena, but she refused to let me pay for them, saying that I had bestowed too many favours upon her, and that I must take them " per amor mio," as she always says. I told her that I could not remember having done anything for her; to which she replied with much solemnity, " But the Lord will remember."

When I pressed her for an explanation, I found that she alluded to my having paid her a moderate price for some plants, which I bought of her when we came here in July. " I bought a bag of meal," she said, " with that money; and we have enjoyed it so much!" She told me that a lady, who passed the summer months near them, had wished to take her for a servant to sweep the house and draw the water. " I was sorry not to go with her," she said. " She was such a sweet good lady!

But when I thought of my mother, I knew that I could not leave her; and when my mother heard of it she said, 'If Polissena goes, we may as well *all* go.'"

I hope I have not tired you with all these little particulars, which do not seem to amount to anything; but you will understand, I never know exactly what you may think of consequence and what not; and so I generally tell you everything, or at least everything which I care about myself. And I have come to care a good deal about Polissena, and I feel as if I always gain something when I am with her. Sometimes I think it is—you remember that our Lord spoke of certain people whom He would *make His abode with*—well, sometimes I think that perhaps she is one of those, and that He is always with her; she seems like it.

August 27th, 1876.—I wanted very much to write this morning, because Polissena passed the day with me yesterday, and told me all the story about the horse. She came in all the rain, dripping wet, but with sunshine enough in her face to illuminate a dozen rainy days, carrying the unfailing basket—potatoes this time, with flowers laid on the top, and chestnut leaves over all.

And after we had made her sit and dry herself a while by the kitchen fire, which she considered quite an unnecessary precaution, I brought her to my room, where we had a long and very interesting conversation. She turned her chair around two or three times at first, and seemed a little uncomfortable as she looked at the pictures on the wall. At last she said to me, "My poor father used to say that it was not proper to turn one's back on any picture of the Lord Jesus or the Madonna; but when they are all round the room, what can I do?"

I managed to set her conscience at rest on this important subject; and then I asked her about the horse who would not drink excepting at the fountain, and she gave me a long and minute horse-biography, of which I will not trouble you with more than a small part. His name was Lilli, and he was a strong, handsome chestnut horse that her father bought just before he died. "He brought us all up," she said; and then, seeing that I looked puzzled at the idea of a horse filling the position of nurse and governess, she explained herself: "He earned the living of all of us when we were children."

She went on to say: "It is true that he would never drink, excepting at the fountain. I could never understand that; who knows what sort of idea he had about it? Perhaps he thought the water in the fountain was cleaner, but I am sure it was not, for I always brought him nice fresh water into the stable. But when he was thirsty he used to call me to take him to the fountain. Sometimes he would call me up in the night, and then if I did not go at once he would call again, and I always knew what he wanted, and could not help going. Poor thing, he was so good, and had done so much for us; we all loved him so much! Besides, if I did not take him to the fountain when he wanted to go, he would not eat either, and then of course we could not expect him to work. He lived with us for more than twenty years, and he was so gentle that he never needed any guiding but my voice; he understood everything I said. Whenever any of us went into the stable he used to make a great many compliments; but more to me than any of the others, because when I went, I always took him a piece of bread or chestnut cake or polenta."

Afterwards I asked her a good many questions about herself and her life, and I was rather surprised, as she is so religious, to find that she does not seem to care much about going to church. She says:—

"I pray better in the forest, and for the most part, while I am at work. I have tried to fall into that habit, because, you know, poor people cannot afford to take a great deal of time for their prayers. With ladies and gentlemen, of course it is different; but I do not think the work makes the prayers any worse. In the forest I am quiet, and nothing disturbs my thoughts; while in church,—well, when I was a child it seems to me that things were different, and that people used to go to church with great devotion: but now, people go in fashionable dresses, and they look about, and whisper, and sometimes they come and whisper to *me;* and then, how can I keep my mind fixed on what is going on?"

To Edwige, who is much troubled with fears of purgatory, she said, "I am never afraid. We must try to do as well as we can; and the Lord will not condemn us; you know what He said, 'Male non fare— paura non avere.'" Which common Italian proverb she fully believes to be of Divine origin.

But if I go on in this way I shall fill up all my letter with Polissena's sayings; so I will leave them, though they are almost all worth remembering. I suppose in everybody's religion one idea, or doctrine rather, takes the lead; in hers it is an overpowering sense of the goodness of the Almighty.

Do you know, Faustina, in the "Roadside Songs," is becoming quite a heroine among the Quakers; and it is really a help and comfort to me to know that some people feel as I do about the army and the conscription, which are eating the heart out of Italy. The Italians have put me down with lofty talk about "l'Amor della patria," and will not understand that it is just because I *do* love Italy that I cannot bear to see it so burdened. These good Quakers want me to write something more about it, but I shall not, for I have not the talent sufficient; and if I had, nobody would mind anything I said. You know I do not believe in the world growing any better,— not until the Lord's kingdom comes.

I was interrupted by the arrival of some friends from Fiumalbo, who always come once a year to pass a day with us. One of them was Rosa Donati, called La Bianca, keeper of the shop where everything is sold in Fiumalbo, from books of devotion to confectionery (of which last she brought us a handsome specimen of her own making, a curious cake which nobody else knows how to make, composed of rice, sugar, and almonds). Her husband is the carpenter, a very poor, humble, hard-working old man, of whom she told us a story yesterday, which made me think that he had really a good deal more idea of " honour " than most of the gentlemen who talk about it, and fight about it.

He has lately, as we already knew, inherited a (for him) considerable property —12,000 francs—from a cousin. But what we did *not* know was, that the cousin made nearly all this money by buying the confiscated Church property for about a tenth of its value. And all this the old carpenter has returned to its original use as nearly as he can, by giving it to his parish priest to use for religious purposes while he lives, and leave to his successor when he dies. So there is a carpenter that I think St. Joseph need not be ashamed of!

To-day Polissena has been to see me again, and, though I did not mean to tell you anything about her in this letter (fearing that you must be tired of hearing about her), she has, in the course of a long conversation, told me some things that throw so much light on her history and character, that I cannot help writing them down now before I forget them.

She says that she had such a good grandmother, who died when she was a little girl, but she can still remember her perfectly. The old lady was very pious and charitable, and would always spare something from her poverty for whoever had need. One day when she was alone in the house with Polissena (then a small child), some one knocked at the door; and she said, "That is a poor beggar; go, my child, and take him a piece of bread!"

But Polissena was unwilling.

"Grandmother, you are *always* sending me to the door with pieces of bread; and pretty soon there will be none left for us!"

"Oh, what a foolish little thing you are!" said the grandmother. "Do you not know that when we help the poor, what goes out at the door always comes back through the window? Nobody ever came to want in that way! But go now, and take the bread to the poor man, and then I will tell you how our Lord knocked at a rich man's door once Himself!"

I will not write out the grandmother's story, because it was a free version of the Madonna and the rich man, with our Lord instead of His mother asking for help; but it made such an impression on Polissena, that she says, "The grandmother never had to speak *twice* to me after that to make me go to the door; indeed, I generally went without being told at all!"

Another little story that the old lady used to tell her children will make you smile if I tell it as Polissena told it, and yet it has a beautiful side to it, and brought the tears to her eyes, and made her voice tremble as she repeated it. "Once it happened that the Lord and St. Peter were walking out together, and they passed through a street in a certain town where some masons were at work on a house, and there was a young man hanging by a rope. You have seen builders tied with ropes in that way, have you not, doing some work on the front of the house? And all at once they heard him exclaim, 'Oh, it is our Lord and St. Peter!'

"And he tried to turn, so as to have a good look at them; and I suppose the rope was not fastened very well; he fell, fell to the ground, and was killed before their eyes! St. Peter was very sad about that poor young man, and he walked on silently for some time, until they found themselves in a wild place, some way out of the city, where there was quite an ugly piece of road, cut like a terrace on the side of the mountain, with a ravine below it full of rocks, and a wood at the bottom, ... really a very dangerous place! A very old man was coming toward them; but as he drew near, his foot slipped, and he rolled down that terrible ravine, among the rocks to the bottom.

"St. Peter supposed, of course, that he was dead; but after a few minutes they saw him climbing up again, and he was hardly hurt at all. And yet it was a much worse fall than the other. St. Peter's heart was still very heavy for the young builder, and he said:

"'Lord, why didst Thou save the old man, whose life is so nearly over, and not the young man, for whom life was just beginning?'

"And our Lord answered:

"'The young man's soul was mine, but the old man's soul is not mine yet!'

"At which answer St. Peter's eyes filled with tears; and that is the reason why, Grandmother said, his eyes have tears in them now, once a year, when his festa comes."

"But, Polissena," I said, after listening to this story, "what do you mean about St. Peter's eyes filling with tears? Do you mean some image of him in a church, or the saint himself in heaven, who sheds tears on his festa?"

"I cannot remember!" she answered; then, after some reflection, "I should not wonder if it were in Rome! It may have been in Rome; it may have been in heaven; but I rather think it was in Rome, because, if it had been in heaven, it would have been difficult for any one to go there and see it, and then come back and tell about it!"

And I have a good deal more to write about the grandmother, but it is growing late, so I think I had better send you the rest in another letter.

I must end Polissena's account of her grandmother, which I left in the middle yesterday.

She went on to say:—

"My grandmother used to sleep with my sister and me—one on each side of her—and before we went to sleep she used to hear us say our prayers, and she would teach us what prayers she knew herself. Sometimes—you know what children are—we were sleepy, and did not want to finish our prayers; but she would say:—

"'You had better go on, children; you

will sleep so much the better, and have such a pleasant awakening in the morning!'

"Poor grandmother, she used to pray so much herself. If we awoke in the night, we would see her, by what light came in through the window, kneeling by an arm-chair that stood by the wall, with a picture of the Madonna hanging over it; I remember just how she looked, always in her night-dress.

"She was often cold at night; and we would call to her:— 'Grandmother, come back to bed! You were cold just now; you told us so; do not stay there in your night-dress!' and she would answer:—

"'I am not cold now, children!'

"She lived to be very old—a lively, pretty old woman, always busy and active, working about the house, and keeping things tidy (for she was extremely **neat in** her ways), and she had hardly any illness before **she died.** Her name was Eulalia; and my mother named **two** children **for her** after she died, **but** neither of them lived long. I suppose we were not worthy to have another Eulalia in the family."

After I had listened to this account, I told Polissena that **it must have been** a great blessing to have such **a good woman in the** family, **to which** she **replied,** quickly, and with a certain **sort of** jealousy that I have often **noticed in** her where her mother is concerned :—

" But **my** mother is so good, too ! In all **my** life I cannot remember that **I ever** heard her speak sharply, **neither have I ever** seen her strike one **of her children.** And I must say that **the children are** good to her. My **brothers** are grown-up men now, but they are always perfectly obedient to her, as if they were little children."

So much then for the family that was brought up by the horse!

I thought you might like to hear these particulars, which, however, I did not mean to make so long; but now I do not mean to trouble you any more about Polissena, excepting that, before I leave her finally, I think I ought to tell you that she has some very peculiar ideas about religion, which I am sure nobody ever taught her, for I never saw them in any religious book, whether Catholic or Protestant. She believes, says she is certain, that there is *no need* of sickness or trouble, and that they only come, in some way or other, from wrong-doing; that if people would trust in the Lord, and leave everything in His hands without fear, and be very careful to "obey Him in everything," as she expresses it, "there is no reason why everybody should not have *two heavens*, one here and the other there."

She added :—

"I always trust the Lord about everything myself; and that *is why* I am so fortunate! When I have no work to do, it never makes me anxious, for I *know* He will think of it; and the day never ends without somebody wanting me for something or other, and sending to hire me. People often wonder at my good fortune, but they could all have just the same if they would!"

There, I have told you enough now (though I will not promise not to have some more to tell you the next time Polissena comes).

CHRIST'S FOLK

IN THE APENNINE.

BY

FRANCESCA ALEXANDER.

EDITED BY

JOHN RUSKIN, D.C.L.,
Honorary Student of Christ Church, and Honorary Fellow of
Corpus Christi College, Oxford.

II.
'PENSATEVI VOI!'

GEORGE ALLEN,
SUNNYSIDE, ORPINGTON, KENT.
1887.

Price One Shilling.

CHRIST'S FOLK

IN THE APENNINE.

REMINISCENCES
OF HER FRIENDS
AMONG THE TUSCAN PEASANTRY.

BY

FRANCESCA ALEXANDER.

EDITED BY
JOHN RUSKIN, D.C.L.,
Honorary Student of Christ Church, and Honorary Fellow of Corpus Christi College, Oxford.

II.
'PENSATEVI VOI!'

GEORGE ALLEN,
SUNNYSIDE, ORPINGTON, KENT.
1887.

Printed by Hazell, Watson, & Viney, Ld., London and Aylesbury.

'PENSATEVI VOI!'

I WANT now to tell you a story that I think will please you; and though not long, it will take me some time to put together all the fragments that I have been able to gather up from Signor Bortolo, and from the present tavern-keeper of Rivalta, Catina's son. I should not have said anything about it if it had not been for what you once wrote—which made a great impression upon me at the time—about the possibility of a tavern being just as good as a church; and so I thought you would like to hear about the only case I ever heard of in which it really was so.

This good Catina—her maiden name was Benetti—came from Asiago, a place beloved alike of geologists and antiquarians, and the old seat of government of the Setti Communi, which kept a sort of half independence for I should be afraid to say how many centuries under the Venetian republic. One of these days, if you care to hear about the strangest and most out-of-the-world corner of the Veneto, I will write you an account of Asiago, where we once stayed for some time. It is enough to say just now that it is a place very remarkable for the piety, honesty, and intelligence of its people.*

Whenever in the Veneto one hears of a parish priest who is doing an extraordinary amount of good, one is extremely likely to

---

* The reader must please observe that in the title of this book, 'Apennine' stands broadly for 'hill country of Italy.'—J. R.

hear in the next breath, 'He came from Asiago! as I have often observed.'

Catina was left an orphan at twelve years old, and went to live with an aunt, whose trade it was to weave and sell linen; and she herself learnt to weave, and did it, as she always did everything, well. Signor Bortolo, who knew her as a middle-aged woman, says that she was very handsome, tall, light in her movements, and very strong: a quite poor photograph which I have of her, taken in extreme old age, and when she was much broken, shows that she had fine regular features, and, apparently, blue eyes and a fair colour.

Francesco Moro, of **Rivalta**, was a raftsman of the Brenta, whose business was to bring loads of wood from the mountains, and sell them in Bassano; and the business carried him every now and then to Asiago. One day he had some money in his pocket, and wanted to buy a piece of linen. Somebody directed him to Catina. She had none on hand, but promised to weave it before his next visit. On his return he found that she had kept her promise; he was pleased with the linen, more pleased with the weaver, and, in his son's words, 'He began then to look upon her with eyes of love.'

They did not waste much time in courtship. He married her without a soldo in her pocket, and took her home to Rivalta, to the house where his father, mother, brother, and brother's wife were all living together. From that day to the end of his life, Francesco Moro seems to have been completely devoted to his wife, and altogether dependent upon her. She was not very happy with his family; she was used to poverty, but not to roughness, and they were,

I fear, rather a rough, hard set of people. As soon as he went away with his raft they set her to bringing loads of wood down from the mountain on her shoulders, as they were in the habit of doing themselves. She had not been used to this sort of work, and it was too hard for her, but they insisted. On the day when her husband was to return they had given her a very heavy load to carry. Her son says:—

She raised it with great difficulty to her shoulder, and it fell off. Then she tried the other shoulder, and it fell again. She tried over and over again in every way she could think of, but she could not carry it, and at last she said, 'I will do this no more!' And she left her bundle of wood and came home without it.

Later in the day, when she saw her husband coming up the bank from the river, she went to meet him, and told him her story, and she said,

'Francesco, help me! If I do this work any longer I shall die!'

He thought a little and then said,

'I *will* help you, but you must do as I say. I will not go home just yet; but you go, and when the supper is ready do not sit down to eat with the others, and do not call me. After supper, prepare something in a tegame* by itself, and call me in, and we will eat together.'

Catina did as she was told, and she and her husband ate together at a table apart after the others had done. The old man took no notice of them until they had finished, then he said,

'I see what you have done, and I know what you mean by it. This is the last meal

* 'Tegame,' an earthen pan.

that you will ever eat in my house. You may sleep here to-night, but in the morning go!'

I have told all this in the words of the son, but now it is easier for me to go on by myself. In the morning the young people went out into the world alone together, without money or provision of any kind; only Catina had a little bundle of clothes that she brought from Asiago. A kind neighbour, to whom they told their story, gave them a breakfast of potatoes, after which they set about making the best of their circumstances, pretty much as a pair of squirrels might have done.

Francesco chose a bit of waste and useless ground, close to the river, to which no one was likely to dispute his right, and there he built with his own hands a shed of rough boards, which for many years was their only shelter summer and winter. There their eleven children were born, and there nearly all the events which I have still remaining to tell you took place. Catina sold most of her clothes, and bought—besides one or two objects of first necessity for the house—two bottles of brandy and a little fruit, with which she opened a shop (*in the shed, of course !*)* The raftsmen and barocciai would not think they could live, and no one else would expect them to live, without a glass of brandy now and then, especially in cold weather. Catina did nothing contrary to her conscience, nor to the conscience of those about her. On the contrary, she was fully persuaded that whatever she did was especially given her to do by the Almighty; so that, in the words of Signor

* Italics mine, and will be mine in future, Francesca never using them.—J. R.

Bortolo, 'She never thought *she* did anything; she thought that God did it all by her means.' Neither was she ever for a moment troubled by their necessities and difficulties.

Her son says of her, that the placidity of her spirit was never disturbed, nor her temper ruffled, by any contrariety; that her face was always smiling and contented. Whenever she undertook any new scheme (and she did undertake a great many, for her poor family) and it did not prosper, she used to say,

'Oh Signore Dio! quest' affare va male. Pensatevi voi!' That is, 'O Lord God! this affair goes badly. See to it Thyself!'

After which she would dismiss the affair from her mind. Her son said:

I have heard her say those words a hundred times; and, whatever the affair was, it *always went well afterwards.*

Her ambition was to sell wine, and how she accomplished it shows just what an energetic woman she was. She had a neighbour, a woman, who owned a little land, and had lately been mowing; this neighbour once told her that she should like to sell her hay. On the next market day, without saying a word to anyone, Catina rose early, went to her friend's hay mow, and took a wisp, only a wisp, of hay; with which she set off before sunrise, for Bassano, twelve miles away,* where she had never been. There she stationed herself among the tents and benches in the Piazza, under the old clock tower, and waited her time.

She did not know a soul in the place, (*which was much more of a great world to*

* And down hill, into the wider world. Asiago is at the head of a sequestered valley.

her than Paris can ever possibly have been to you); but she was not at all anxious, and did not trouble herself to speak to any one. It was God's business, no hers, to provide for the husband who had sacrificed everything for her, and for the babes in the shed by the Brenta. She thought that He had sent her down to Bassano to sell hay that morning; and of course, all in good time, He would send somebody to buy it. Pretty soon, Count Niccolo Caffo, one of the principal men of Bassano, strayed out through the market, and his attention was attracted by the silent, stately woman, standing still like a statue, while the others were shouting and gesticulating to attract attention and invite customers. He went up to her, and asked what she wanted. She answered that she had come from the country to sell hay, bringing a specimen with her. At this he told her that he thought they might make a bargain, as he just then wanted some hay for his horses. And he invited her into his house near by, that they might come to an agreement regarding the price, etc. When there, she told him that her great wish was to sell the hay for a barrel of wine; at which he at first laughed, the wine (of which he had a good store, made on his own estate,) being worth much more than the hay. But Catina had something about her, which I, having never seen her, cannot attempt to describe, (but which, as you know well, some people *do* have,) which generally made everybody do exactly what she said. And when Count Caffo had finished laughing, the next thing he did was to promise that he would on the following day send the barrel of wine to Rivalta, and take away the hay. 'Catina walked home, quite contented, and immediately went to the house of her neighbour who owned the hay.

'I have sold your hay,' she said, 'for a barrel of wine; and now I want you to wait a little for your money. Let me keep the wine, and sell it in my shop; and when it is sold, I will pay you all.'

To this her friend readily consented; Catina sold her wine, paid for it, and had a fair profit left; and better than that, she had made a good friend in Count Caffo, whose kindness from that day forth never failed her. He presented her to his friend, Signor Ambrogio Zanchetta, the father of Signor Bortolo, and brother of our dear 'Mother of the orphans;'[*] a man whose memory is still held in great reverence in Bassano. Signor Ambrogio immediately lent her another barrel

[*] I hope to give her story in next number.

of wine, and a sack of Indian corn, to be paid for after she had sold them. And it soon became well known that everybody could trust Catina; her debts were always paid when due, and no one ever lost by her. Her husband meanwhile kept on with his raft and his loads of wood; but such was his confidence in her, that he always left whatever money he earned in her hands, reserving only, as his son said, "a few coppers to give to the poor, when he went to church." (By the way, do you not think that almost any man in his position would have thought that *he* was one of the poor himself, and rather have expected people to give to *him?*)

After a while the neighbours began to tell old Moro, the father, that it was a shame in him never to help his son Francesco; and finally the old man was shamed into giving him a very small bit of land, consisting of a steep bank, sloping *down* from a terraced mountain road. Catina, immediately on coming into possession of this handsome and unexpected fortune, proposed to her husband that they should build a tavern! And they really did it! Without spending money, or hiring workmen, husband, wife, and larger children all worked together. None of them knew anything about building, but somehow they *did* build it, and not so badly, either!

Catina *made the mortar, carried stones, and directed everything.* When the building was finished, it consisted of three rooms, one above the other; of which the highest only, where the shop was kept, was on a level with the road, and the other two were built into, (or hollowed out of,) the bank.

And now I come to what I particularly

wanted to tell you,—the very peculiar way in which Catina carried on a tavern, and kept shop. First of all, I ought to say that it was a very successful way. She died quite rich, according to her ideas, and her son is now a very prosperous tavern-keeper, who cannot speak of his mother without his voice trembling, and his eyes filling with tears. But it *was* a peculiar way. The first thing she did was, to make every Saturday a great kettle of soup, and give it all to the poor. Her children remonstrated,—'Mother, we have not bread enough to eat; and you give soup to the poor!' She answered, 'God gives everything to us, and we can give nothing to Him! Only He has said to us, that what we give to the poor, we give to Him; let me give back to Him a little of what is His own!'

Still the children would not be contented; and they teased her so, for what they considered her extravagance, that, for once in her life, she yielded, and on the next Saturday there was no more soup for the poor. On the afternoon of the same day, a contadino came to the shop, to settle some affair with Catina; and while he was talking with her, his donkey, which he had left outside with the cart, put his head in at the shop window, and somehow managed to upset a large basket of eggs, there exposed for sale. Catina, on seeing what had happened (a considerable misfortune for her), said:

'See, children; you would not let me make the soup for the poor, and now this misfortune has happened! The price of those eggs would have paid for twenty kettles of soup!'

And from that day forth the children let her give away what she liked in peace; and the poor never wanted again for their Saturday's dinner.

When she went to Bassano, which she always did, I believe, on market day, the first thing she did was to go to church, and give the priest three *lire Venete*, to say a mass for the souls in purgatory. To this mass she listened with great devotion; then went about her affairs, with the full assurance that the blessing of heaven went with her. As I have said, her temper was of the sweetest and most tranquil; but there were two things which, with all her power of endurance, she could never bear,—profanity, or evil speaking. If any man, talking with others in her little shop, so far forgot himself as to use the name of the Almighty without due reverence, or tell any story injurious to the character of a neighbour, Catina, in unspeakable distress and agitation, would take him by the jacket and put him out of the door, saying:

'Not here! For the love of God, not here!'

(All this, you understand, at the risk of losing her customers; but in Catina's manner of doing business, the affairs of the other world were always first, and those of this world second.)

And having noticed that, in other osterie, as the men sat around the fire after eating and drinking, their conversation was seldom free from profane language and scandalous stories, she, in building *her* little tavern, would have no seats in the chimney; saying that *her fire was for cooking*, and not for people to sit and gossip over.

Her son and Signor Bortolo both agreed in telling me that prayer was such a constant habit with her, that there was hardly any time when she was not praying. Often when people came into her shop to buy, they found her so absorbed in prayer that she did not even see them.* When they had aroused her attention, and she was weighing out the bread, or fruit, or whatever they wanted, she talked to them always of God.

Signor Bortolo says of her: 'She mixed God in everything: she could not

---

* The reader will please observe that whatever the truth of the Bible may be, he may learn from these stories the accurate meaning of it. These two first given explain what St. Paul (or whoever else wrote them) *meant* by the verses, 'Rejoice evermore,' 'Pray without ceasing,' 'In *everything* give thanks; for this is the will of God, in Christ Jesus, concerning you.'

make a bargain for a bag of Indian corn without mixing Him in it!'

She was often at his house, when he was a child (for the Caffo and Zanchetta families continued until the end of her life her best friends); and as she entered the cortile where he was generally playing with his brother and sisters, she never saluted them in any usual fashion, but always with the words,

'Keep close to God, children; He does everything!'

The thought that He was always with her, made her never afraid to undertake anything of which she saw the need, however difficult. There was no church in her time at Rivalta, and one seemed to be much wanted. She proposed to the few people of the village that they should build one; and such was her influence over them, that they immediately set about it, she working among them, as she had done at the building of her tavern, and all her family, large and small, helping.

When the church was finished, the good Signor Ambrogio presented an altar cloth and two candlesticks. *And this church is at present maintained by the Rivalta people, but principally by Catina's son, who, in piety, seems to follow his mother very closely.* Catina lived to be very old ; nobody ever knew exactly *how* old. During the last years of her life she became infirm and quite deaf ; but (her son said) she looked and seemed perfectly happy, 'praying always, and knitting always ; sitting until the end in the corner of the shop where she had sat ever since her youth, with a very bright, sweet look in her face!'

She died in 1872, her husband having passed away several years before.

There is my story; not just what it might have been if I had known Catina myself, but still, I think you will say, worth the time it will take you to read it.

Yes, Francesca, that is all very well; but you don't count how many times some of us may want to read it over again; and then to think over it; and then to read the history, if we can find it anywhere, of the Seven Commonwealths under the rule of Asiago,—of which I am sure we shall be grateful for whatever you will take patience to tell us. But chiefly, for myself, I want to know of the Eleven who built the Tabernacle, what has become of the Ten little Franks and Catinas who were thus brought up, at home,—as it is more and more my notion that children should always be, and none of them sent to schools or lycées, other than their parents can provide. But I say nothing till Francesca tells us how the people of Asiago remained so pious, intelligent, and honest; and what has become of the Ten little Cats and their tribes.

BRANTWOOD,
February 11*th*, 1887.

CHRIST'S FOLK

IN THE APENNINE.

BY
FRANCESCA ALEXANDER.

EDITED BY
JOHN RUSKIN, D.C.L.,
Honorary Student of Christ Church, and Honorary Fellow of Corpus Christi College, Oxford.

III.
THE MOTHER OF THE ORPHANS.

GEORGE ALLEN,
SUNNYSIDE, ORPINGTON, KENT.
1887.

Price One Shilling.

CHRIST'S FOLK

IN THE APENNINE.

REMINISCENCES

OF HER FRIENDS
AMONG THE TUSCAN PEASANTRY.

BY

FRANCESCA ALEXANDER.

EDITED BY

JOHN RUSKIN, D.C.L.,

Honorary Student of Christ Church, and Honorary Fellow of Corpus Christi College, Oxford.

III.

THE MOTHER OF THE ORPHANS.

GEORGE ALLEN,
SUNNYSIDE, ORPINGTON, KENT.
1887.

Printed by **Hazell, Watson,** & *Viney, Ld., London and Aylesbury.*

THE MOTHER OF THE ORPHANS.

I THINK we are beginning, Francesca and I, perhaps a little too grandly with our Polissenas, and Catinas, and Superioras, all at once. Here are two letters just come, one from Francesca herself, one from her mother, which describe another order of folk of the Apennine,—they also very sweet, and dear, and wonderful; and to be kept reverent record of, among the servants of heaven. So we will let the story of the Superiora wait a little, and have some talk of these, only first, here is what Francesca says in answer to the envoi of "Pensatevi" and its questions :—

"But now I must thank you for the beautiful words that you have written at the end of 'Pensatevi voi!' especially for what you said about schools. I have a perfect horror, myself, of all 'institutions' which separate children from their families; and I, too, have known young people who have learnt infidelity, and much else that is bad, in those places. But one lesson they never fail to learn, whatever else is wanting,—that they can do very well without papa and mamma; and this lesson, once learnt, is never again forgotten, as papa and mamma, after they grow old, usually find out. And I do think that parents must be very bad indeed, not to be better, for their children, than any one else.

"Then I wonder what most people mean by *education*. Awhile ago, I heard somebody lamenting sadly about a dear little girl whom I know, that her education was interrupted by her care of a sick mother! The poor mother wrote me, about the same time, that she could never be thankful enough for the blessing that she had in her little daughter, *who never forgot anything that could be a comfort to her.* I wonder if she would have been taught that, or anything else as good, in a boarding-school?

"But how my pen is running away with me to-day! Worse than ever before, I think. Next week I will send you a letter all about Asiago and the Sette Communi: I do not write it to-day, because I want a little time to think up my recollections. Meanwhile, your wish to know about the 'little cats, and their tribes,' obliges me to tell you what I fear it will make you sad to hear,—that nearly all Catina's children died young, though not in infancy. People say, 'They were taken away early, in mercy to their good mother, because the world is so wicked now! Who knows, if they had lived, if they could have resisted.' Of her six sons, only one is left; and he, a gray-haired man, the good tavern-keeper of Rivalta. He told me that he had three sisters living, two married, and one single; but I have never seen any of them.

"I wonder at your little girls not caring for botany,* which I have always found delightful, though I have never had much time to study it: and I wonder especially

---

* In answer to a word in my last letter about my Saturday class, of which I will give some account in next number. Their attention was, at the time, restricted to cress and cabbage, and not permitted to wander towards wild and useless things like wall-flowers!

that, among the cruciferæ flowers, not one of them thought of wall flowers, my own favourite!

"Now, I want to tell you that I feel so much obliged to you for putting it into my head to draw these pictures of Saints!* It is the pleasantest work that ever I did, and keeps me always in good company; and I have many beautiful stories that no one now seems to know anything about. Paolina comes to me once a week, and I have chosen her as a model for a lady who especially practised the virtue of patience, because I think she looks like the character. I asked her the other day if she had ever, in her life, been out of temper, and she had to think a great while before she could re-

---

* In sequel to "Roadside Songs," and illustrating more authentic traditions.

member, but finally was rather of opinion that she had been, some time or other."

(Now we come to the other orders of Christ's Folk.)

"Do you know, your interest in my bee, and in Marietta's swallows, makes me want to tell you about some other pretty creatures that I have been fond of. I have had very few pets in my life, if that means animals of my own to take care of; but I have had a good many four-footed friends; and I am going to leave now several things that I wanted very much to write, for the sake of telling you about a cow that I used to know a great many years ago, when we first began to go to L'Abetone. Not that there is much to tell, only she was rather a remarkable character, and she and I were greatly attached to each other. She was one of five, that used to go about the country attended by a poor girl, generally considered to be under-witted. Marina was the girl's name,* and she was certainly rather silly, and not just like other people; but she was affectionate, and usually gentle, though she would fly into a terrible passion if any one teased her cows; and she had a poetical streak in her nature, that made me like to talk to her. She loved those cows with an absolutely passionate affection. I remember her saying to me once, 'Poor cows! they are a great deal better than we are. I am sure that God must

---

* In order to prepare for general index, I think it will be best henceforward to put a terminal note to each part of " Folk," with the names of the people in it. Here are our old friend Paolina, and a Marietta and Marina, all worth our memory, in two pages. So I shall introduce at once the proposed registry, which must be also a dictionary: for I suppose Paolina means little Paula, and Marietta little Mary; but Marina, sea-maid (?)—as Marino Faliero.

love them more than He does us, because they never do any harm, nor speak evil of their neighbours!' She treated them always with the most deferential politeness, and had given them very poetical names. They were, Bella Rosa, Stella, Damigella, Argentina, and Galantina. And, like most animals so treated, they had become almost human in intelligence and power of affection. Cows have their sympathies, like the rest of us, and for some reason best known to herself, Argentina saw fit to attach herself to me. She was a very beautiful young creature, not quite full grown, with a quiet and stately grace about her that would have done credit to any lady. She was snow white; only the tips of her horns, the tassel at the end of her tail, her hoofs, and her heavy fringes of eyelashes, were black. And,—I am afraid you will find it hard to believe what I am going to say, but Mammina remembers it as well as I do,—when I was drawing in the field, as I often did in those days, Argentina would come behind me, bend her beautiful head until it rested on my shoulder, and watch, with much apparent interest, the progress of my work! Mammina was frightened at first to see those long horns so near my eyes; but the gentle creature was always careful not to hurt any one. And Mammina has always believed that she really cared for what I was doing, and liked to see the picture grow under my hand. I suppose it was only the wish to share in whatever I was doing, that one often sees in animals toward those whom they love.

"But I did not think this would have been so long a story; you must excuse it. And now I must end, for it is growing late. Mammina wrote you a letter yesterday, which, I am sorry to say, I forgot to post, so now I must send them both at once. Good-bye. I wish I had more time and more paper. With love as ever.

"FLORENCE, *March* 10*th*, 1887."

(Here follows the ratification by Mammina in quite good time.)

"The beautiful milk-white cow, when she stood behind F. and rested her chin on her shoulder, certainly had every appearance of watching the landscape, and the gradual creation of it on the paper. I, also, had a friend among them, but mine was a cream colour, finished with black. Their mistress was half-poetess and half-underwitted; she was the woman who, when her baby died, said she meant to have given it to Francesca when it was two years old. We used to buy a great dish of salt, and go to meet the cows as they were going home at sundown, and give it to them. They were so fond of it. One evening the cream-coloured one—her name was Bella Rosa—left the others, and walked home with us. She was a splendid creature in her way, with all the beauty of young wild life, and grown in mountain air. We passed through the fir-trees, and came to the fountain. Mr. Alexander had amused himself, helped by all the boys in Abetone, in making a wall of earth, covered with turf full of flowers, where the water ran from the brim of the basin; so it had made a transparent little lake, a few inches deep. Into this Bella Rosa walked, and after standing a moment, dropped her head till it just touched the water, drinking it so gently that it was not disturbed; she seemed rather breathing than drinking; and all the time she watched us with her great wild soft eyes. It was just sundown; it had been raining, and had cleared; the sky was pale transparent blue, cloudless, but the mists were drifting down the ravines, rose colour, white, and grey, fire colour prevailing.

"We had a tame canary that appeared also to like to see F. draw. Mr. A. found it at Bellosguardo; it had dropped into the road from a nest above a high wall; he brought it home, and we brought it up. It was summer time, the windows were all open, but it always kept in or about the house, and made itself entirely one of the family. It came to the table and breakfasted with us; it went with us when we walked out, flying from tree to tree, so as to keep near us; at night it roosted on the bar of the bed; it had no name but Birdie, but always answered when I called him, even when he was out of sight. One day I saw him on a fir-tree, and a cat creeping about it; I went to it and called him, and he flew down to my hand. He used to sit on the handle of F.'s pen and see her draw, and when she threw him off, he would make a circle round the room, and alight again on the pen-handle. How much he comprehended, we could never fancy, but all creatures have a wonderful sympathy with human beings.

"Do you know you are decidedly gaining health and strength? I cannot remember when the winter has dealt with you so kindly. Take good care of yourself, the greatest care, is the serious charge of

"LA TUA MAMMINA.

"FLORENCE, *March* 16*th*, 1887."

I must yet find room, before we come to the Superiora, for the story of Lilla with the blue eyes, with its incidental description of the King of Italy, better than any that got into the papers.

"But I wish that you could have seen how many people have come to me with sad faces and gone away with happy ones, in these last few weeks! One morning, when I went upstairs, I found waiting outside my door a girl whom I used to know, years ago, on a farm at Bellosguardo, as a pretty, barefoot baby, just large enough to toddle along by my side, and help me pick flowers, when I went to walk with her little black-eyed cousin, Frederico, just the same size. Lilla had blue eyes of extraordinary size and colour, with black, curling lashes; so that we have always spoken of her, ever since, as the baby with the blue eyes. And poor Frederico—he never grew to be anything but a baby! He was taken away suddenly, one April day, before the flowers had faded that he had gathered that morning, 'to give to the Signorina,' as he said. And Lilla grew up to a woman, and lost her parents, and made what was called a prosperous marriage, with a Florentine shopkeeper, who fell in love with her blue eyes. And then he was unfortunate in business, and they became poor, and poorer still, until at last, there she was waiting at my door, with a handful of flowers and a baby. So I asked them in; and when they had sat down, I saw that Lilla was in trouble, and that she was afraid to tell me what it was. She could only tremble and hold down her head. So I began to question her, and told her not to be frightened, but to tell me just what was the matter. Still she could not speak, and I said, 'But I know that you are in trouble; I see by your eyes that you have shed many tears.' 'Yes,' she answered, 'I cried all last night.' 'Then tell me what the matter is!' and at last it all came out with a sob: 'We cannot pay the rent! The landlord is going to turn us out!' I was a good deal relieved to find out that this was all, and told her not to worry any more about that, but to tell me how much they were owing. But this she would not do, saying that the debt was *too large*, and that all she wished was that I would give her a little help for the present. However, I pressed her, and at last, dropping her face very low, and twisting her fingers very hard, she said, under her breath, '*Twenty francs.*' 'Now, Lilla,' said I, 'I do not think you are telling me the truth; the debt is more than twenty francs; tell me just what it is.' And, raising her eyes to my face with a sort of desperation she said, 'Well then, *twenty-five!*' But I do not believe there was a lighter heart in Florence that day than Lilla's (unless it was mine), when she went away with the money in her pocket.

"But it is rather hard to keep one's patience with the doings of the municipality just now, pulling down old houses before new ones are built, and making everybody generally uncomfortable. I have to think very often about that text that forbids our speaking evil of the rulers of our people; only I should like to know who they are; there never seems to be exactly anybody responsible. I am sure I like the King and Queen,—every one does; but it is hardly fair to call them rulers, when they cannot have so much their own way as other people. Sometimes the King will insist on having his a little, about his own affairs; he did last year, when the cholera was about, and everybody tried to make him stay out of danger. I saw a lady a little while ago, married to a Piedmontese, who was at Busca, just where the cholera was worst, last summer, when the King went there, and she gave me an interesting account of it all. She said every one was in a panic, and afraid to go near the sick people; but the King took hold as if he had been an hospital nurse, going always where the danger was greatest, sitting by the beds of the sick, administering their medicines, rubbing them with spirit when the chill came, giving food, advice, or money as they were wanted, sometimes sympathising, sometimes laughing and jesting, to keep up their hearts, until others came forward to help, just for shame. And in the evening, when he went to rest tired out, and his servants came about him to change his clothes and 'fumigate' him, he used to smile at their anxieties, and then raise his eyes to heaven, as if to say, 'There is where my safety comes from!' Of course all this did not suit every one, and there was some talk of passing a law to prevent 'sovereigns' from risking their lives; but Umberto said if they did he should be the first to break it, and as every one knew that he would keep his word, there was no more said about it.

"Mammina has just been reading your 'Unto This Last,' and said so much to me about it that I *stole* a few minutes for it this morning (and was sorry I could not steal more). She and I were both much impressed by what you said, that masters should treat their workmen as they would be willing to have their own children treated if they were in the same place. Do you know, it is *exactly* what I have heard her say, ever since I was a little child,—not about workmen (of whom she never had any experience), but *servants*. And neither she nor I ever heard such a word from any one else, and people have generally looked upon her ideas as very visionary; but she has always acted upon them, and nobody ever had such devoted servants. So if you want to know the practical working of your doctrine, I will tell you what Edwige said, after twenty years' service in our house. Some girls in my room were talking about an acquaintance who had just inherited a great fortune, and one of them said to Edwige, jestingly, 'If any one should leave you so much money, what would you do with it?' And she answered, without a moment's hesitation, 'I would keep on doing the work here, just the same, only then *I would not be paid for it.*'

"In one thing, Mammina says, perhaps you may think that she goes too far.* She thinks that servants should be paid enough to enable them to lay by a provision for their old age, without being dependent on the charity even of their employers; and she thinks, if people cannot afford to do this, they should keep fewer servants, or live in more humble style in other respects.

"FLORENCE, *March 16th*, 1885."

---

* Mammina *has* a way sometimes of going too far, certainly! But not in this instance.—J. R.

After this lovely picture of the King of Italy, how well comes this following, of one of her truest nobles!

The Mother of the Orphans.

In the beautiful city of Bassano, on the Brenta, between the mountains and the plain, Signora Maria Zanchetta has passed the eighty-five years of her busy, happy, and useful life, bringing a blessing to all who have come near her, first in her own family, and afterwards, for the last forty-five years, to one generation after another of poor orphan girls, to whom she has been more than a mother. She always had, from childhood, as she herself told me, a wish to enter a religious life; but her vocation seems to have been rather for the active than for the contemplative life.

She belongs to an honourable family of

Bassano, and appears to have had an especial love and reverence for her parents, whom she would never leave as long as they lived. After their death she continued to live with an invalid sister, Paola, whom she remembers always with great tenderness, and who is spoken of still, by those who knew her, as something very near a saint. I have often wondered how much of Signora Maria's sweet and beautiful Christian spirit, which has brought comfort into hundreds of lives, may be owing to the influence of the saintly elder sister, whose helpless condition must have made her seem, to herself and others, comparatively useless in the world, but who lived always so very near to heaven!

After Paola died, Maria, being no longer needed at home, resolved to give herself entirely to some charitable work, and her mind turned to the girls' orphan asylum, close to her own house. Her brother, and other relations, would have preferred that she should have become a nun in one of those convents where girls of noble families are sent for education, considering that such a life was more honourable, and better suited to her condition. She told me this part of her story herself, and added:

"In the convent I should have been paid for my work, but I wanted to serve the Lord without recompense in this world, and so I came here to the orphans."

There she has lived ever since, *wearing the same dress as the poor girls*, living their life, entering into all their pleasures and troubles; *overseeing the washing, giving a hand to the mending*, leading a humble, laborious life, full, one would think, of wearisome cares and burdens,—a mother's burdens, without a mother's instinct to support them; but still, if one may judge by her face, she has lived in perpetual sunshine. And how young she looks still! She must have been a delicate blonde beauty in her youth; and she still retains a complexion like a sweetbriar rose, and her kind blue eyes are as clear and peaceful as an infant's. Her hair, still abundant as in youth, is quite white, and yet not like snow, unless it be snow with the evening sunshine upon it; one sees in a moment that it has once been golden, and it is finer than anything that I ever saw, excepting thistledown. Her dress is of the poorest and plainest, and yet I cannot feel that she would be more beautiful in any other. A blue cotton dress, and cap of the same, with a handkerchief and apron such as are worn by the contadine,—nothing else; but all arranged with scrupulous neatness. There is nothing monastic in the dress, nor in the life ; Signora Maria is free to stay or go as she will ; she is bound by no vow, belongs to no order ; there has been nothing but the love of God and of the poor children to hold her to her place all these long years. She has some property, but *she leaves the use of it to her family,** taking for herself only just what is sufficient for her own maintenance in the asylum, that she may not take anything from the orphans.

I had long wished to know this good Signora Maria ; and finally, last May, I had the great pleasure of seeing her. I had sent to ask at what hour she could see me ; to which she replied, "Any time after six in the

---

* How many, so-called, Reformations, disruptions, dishonours, and agonies of the Catholic Church would have been spared her, had the Popes simply insisted on this law being observed by her religious orders !—J. R.

morning." Which I thought was pretty well for eighty-five! When, the next morning, I went with Edwige to the orphan asylum, and we entered the very modest little "bottega," as they call it, with its low ceiling, and counter where they sell artificial flowers, and certain simple medicines of their own preparing in which the Bassano people have great faith: and where also they receive orders for ornamental laundry-work, and for embroidery of a religious description;—when, as I was saying, we entered this room, half a dozen elderly women were standing talking together, all in the same old-fashioned blue dresses. I asked if I could see the Superiora, on which this very pretty and young-looking lady came forward; and I, not dreaming that she could be the aged saint for whom I was looking, repeated my question. "A servirla!" she replied. I was obliged to explain the astonishment which I could not conceal, by saying that I had expected to see a much older lady. "I *am* old," she answered, "but I have good health, thank the Lord!" And then she led us through a room where a number of girls were doing the peculiar laundry-work of which I have spoken. One cannot call it ironing, for no iron is used about it; but with their fingers, and a fine stick kept for the purpose, they work the starched linen into all kinds of delicate patterns.

They all rose and bowed politely as we passed, and then the old lady preceded us up the stone staircase (which she mounted so rapidly that she left me some way behind her), and conducted us to a pleasant upper chamber, where we all sat down together. On this day, and on those following, when I was taking her portrait, I gathered many particulars of her own life, and also about the institution, which I must write down one by one as I can remember them, for I find it impossible to arrange them in any order.

She told me that they were in all seventy-five, between women and girls. Every girl taken into the institution has a right to a home in it for life, if she will; and many never choose to leave it, or if they do, they return to it; but others have married, or gone to service, or to live with their relations. Once, many years ago, she had seven little slave girls put temporarily under her care by a good missionary who had bought them in Africa. She seems to have a peculiar tenderness in her remembrance of the poor little unbaptized savages. "The others call me Superiora," she said, "but *they* used to call me Mamma Maria."

And her voice softened to more than its usual gentleness as she said those words.

And now I must leave the dear old lady for a moment, to repeat what Silvia told me once, about those same little slave girls.

It was a warm summer's evening, and Silvia and I were sitting, as we often do, on the broad stone steps of the Rezzonico Palace, between the two immense old stone lions that guard the door, and watching the sunset behind the mountains. And Silvia was telling me how, when she was a very small child, those little African girls were brought to the house, and what wild black faces they had, and what brilliant eyes. As they were running about the wide lawn behind Palazzo Rezzonico (which stands in a retired country place about a mile from the city), they caught sight of those stone lions by the door, and immediately pressed about them, *and fell to embracing them as if they had been dear friends, and covered them with tears and kisses;** and Silvia thought they were thinking of their own country, and perhaps of lions which they had seen in their African deserts. I asked Signora Maria if she knew what had become of those poor girls. She said that she had heard that two of them afterwards entered a convent; but she had lost sight of them all for many years, and indeed they had only remained in Bassano for five months.

While I was drawing the old lady's portrait, a tall, strong, very pleasant-looking woman, of fifty or so, came in and stood beside me. She wore the same dress as the Superiora, excepting that she had no cap, nor other

---

* I think this is the loveliest thing I ever heard of the relations between animals and man.—J. R.

covering for her wavy black hair, which was elaborately braided, and knotted up behind, in the fashion commonly followed by the contadine in this part of the country. She had very bright eyes, in which a smile seemed to have taken up its permanent abode, even when the rest of her face was serious. Her voice was soft (there seems to be something in the atmosphere of that house which makes everybody's voice soft); but her movements were rapid and energetic, and she evidently had a supply of vigour and spirit sufficient for half-a-dozen, at least, of average women. She was extremely interested in the progress of the picture, (which she said was as much like the Superiora as anything could be that was *sitting still*,) but it was rather a grievance to her that the old lady *would* be taken in her homely house dress.

"Come now, you *might** wear that other cap!" she said, bending over the little fair Superiora, putting her strong arm very softly around her neck, and speaking coaxingly as if to a baby; then looking at me: "She has such a pretty cap, that I made up for her myself, and she will not wear it!"

"I wear it when I go out," said Signora Maria, "but I would rather have my likeness in the dress that I always wear at home."

I too said that I would rather draw her just as she was.

"I suppose you are right," said the younger woman, regretfully, "but she is so much prettier in that cap!"

I thought her quite pretty enough in the old blue cap, and kept on with my work. Meanwhile I asked some questions about the institution. Signora Maria said that it

---

* These three last flashes of italic are F.'s.—J. R.

was founded in the last century by a good priest, Don Giorgio Pirani, and afterwards further endowed by Don Marco Cremona, whom she had herself known in his old age. How old this Don Marco was she could not remember; a cast of his face, which she afterwards showed me, and which she told me was taken after his death, represented a very handsome, benevolent-looking man, of about seventy; but I imagine (judging from the rest of the conversation) that he must have been much older. She told me that the founder, Don Giorgio, having inherited considerable property, and having no relations that needed it, had bought the land, and three or four houses, which he had thrown into one, and had given it all for poor orphan girls of Bassano. The place accommodates seventy-five girls and women, and is always full. Thirty centimes (3d.) a-day are allowed for the maintenance of each girl, and were probably sufficient in Don Giorgio's time, but times have changed since then. However, they do various kinds of work, principally of a religious or ecclesiastical nature,—making priests' dresses, or artificial flowers for the altar, or wafers to be used at the Communion; besides sewing, knitting, and embroidery of all kinds;—and the women work for the children, and the whole seventy-five live together in one affectionate and united family. The old lady seemed very fond of her "tose," as she calls the girls, and said that they also loved her; which I should think they would, for a more entirely lovable woman it would be hard to find. She has the delightful manners of an old-fashioned Venetian, full of grace, sweetness, and vivacity, and would think that she failed in one of the first

Christian duties if she did not observe all the laws of politeness. She never once failed, during our rather frequent visits at the institution, to come downstairs to meet us, receiving me always at the outside door with a kiss on both cheeks; and when we came away she would accompany us into the cortile, and stand there taking leave with the sun on her white hair. When however she found that this last attention made me really uncomfortable, she desisted; for her politeness being rather of the heart than of etiquette, she never fails in comprehending and considering the feelings of those about her.

But to return to our conversation. The woman with the black wavy hair, whose name was, as I found out, Annetta, remarked with regard to the good Don Giorgio Pirani, that "he died so young, poor man!"

As it seemed he had accomplished a great deal in his life, I was rather surprised, and asked, "How young?" To which she replied, in a tone of deep compassion, "Only seventy-five, poor man! But then he had worn himself out with the care of the institution, and he had a great deal of trouble."

Annetta calculated age in the Bassano fashion: in this healthy air, and with the usually simple habits of life of the people, longevity is the rule and not the exception. The portrait of Don Giorgio's mother hangs beside his in the refectory, with an inscription stating that it was painted "in the year of her age eighty-nine;" also that her name was Daciana Pirani, and that she assisted her two sons, Giorgio and Santi, in their charitable work for the orphans. The picture itself bears the date 1774, and represents a fresh-coloured, erect, and very pleasant-looking lady, with bright black eyes ; very plainly dressed in a long-waisted brown gown and blue apron, with a little dark-coloured cap, which time has rendered so indistinct that I cannot quite make out the fashion of it. A plain handkerchief, apparently of fine white linen, is folded over her bosom, and her arms are bare to the elbows, with a fine Venetian gold chain wound several times around one of them,— her only ornament, excepting her little round earrings. She is standing by a table, on which are her crucifix, prayer-book, and rosary. The Superiora told me that when Don Giorgio was engaged in building and fitting up his asylum, sometimes, at the table, his mother would observe that he was absent and low-spirited, and had little appetite ; at which she would ask him anxiously, "What ails you, my son?" and he would reply, "I have no more money for my workmen." At this she always said, "Oh, if that is all, do not be troubled; I will see to it;" and rising from the table she would leave the room, to return in a few minutes with a handful of money sufficient for the immediate expenses. Don Giorgio himself must have had, if his portrait tells the truth, a singularly kind, sensible, and cheerful face, with more regular beauty than Don Marco Cremona, but less imposing, with dark eyes and white curling hair.

Of Santi Pirani I could learn nothing, excepting that he was a priest, an excellent man, and his brother's helper.

But to return to what I was saying about the Bassano fashion of reckoning age. It is not long since a Bassano gentleman, himself quite a wonderful picture of vigorous health, was complaining to me that the health of the city was not what it used to be.

"Indeed," he said, with the air of one bringing forward an unanswerable proof of his assertion, "at this present time, among all my acquaintances, I know only one man past a hundred! My father knew several; but now, they all seem to drop off between eighty and ninety!" And he shook his head sadly.

I asked some questions about his centenarian friend, and was told that he was a poor man, and lived on charity.

"We all give to him," he said: "he always worked as long as he could, and at his age we do not think it ought to be expected of him."

As nearly as I can understand, people here begin to be considered elderly when they are about eighty, but those who die before ninety are thought to have died untimely.

Signora Maria's family had an old servant, by name Bortolo Mosca, who lived with them for seventy-two years. He entered their service at fourteen, and left it—for a better world, I hope—at eighty-six. He was quite feeble for some time before he died, and his master kept a servant expressly to wait upon him.

A woman servant, Maria Cometa, died in their house at nearly the same age, having passed all her life in their service.

I was much interested in observing Annetta's behaviour to her Superiora; it was half reverential, half caressing; I could hardly tell whether she considered the old lady as a patron saint, or a pet child. Anxious to know what was the tie between them, I asked Annetta how long she had been in the place. She did a little ciphering on her fingers, and then said, "Forty years." In answer to other questions, she told me that her father and mother had both died, within a few weeks of each other, when she was a small child, the youngest of seven; and her uncle, finding himself left with the burden of so large a family on his shoulders, had thought well to relieve himself in part by putting the smallest and most helpless "with the orphans." "*She* has been my mother ever since," she said, dropping her voice, and laying her hand on the little old lady's shoulder. She added that some of her brothers had come on in the world, and had wished to take her home, and that she had gone at various times and stayed in their families; but that she had always come back to her place in the institution, because she could never be happy, for any length of time, anywhere else.

I asked if the girls whom they took in were generally good, and repaid their kindness as they should do; to which the old lady replied, "Many of them do, and are a great comfort; but others give us much trouble. What can we do? We must have patience, we are here on purpose." "Besides," said Annetta, cheerfully, "it would never do for us to have all our reward in this world; if we did, we could not expect any on the other side."

The Superiora told me many interesting stories about the institution, and of the bequests that had been left to it by various Bassano families, of which the most valuable appeared to be some land in the country, with one or two contadine houses, where the girls are sent occasionally to pass a day in the open air, and enjoy themselves. Many families had bequeathed furniture and pictures to the institution, so that one sees everywhere massive nut-wood chairs, and tables carved and inlaid, all of old republican times. One picture, of which I do not recollect the date, but it is about two hundred years old, I should think, represents a young lady with fair curls, magnificently dressed in brocade and jewels, by name Maddalena Bernardi, who looks always as if wondering at the simple unworldliness of the life about her; and beside her hangs the last of her race, (her son, I suppose, for he is much like her in feature; but no one knows, now;) a poor Franciscan frate, ". who did a great deal for the orphans," Signora Maria says. Next to the frate, between him and good Don Giorgio, she showed me a Venetian senator, all robe and wig, with a face looking like nobody in particular, scarlet drapery tossed about in confusion, and a background of very black thunderclouds. "This picture," she said, "was left us by the Doge Erizzo, and represents one of his family: he left us also a hundred and twenty staia of Indian corn, and two barrels of wine, yearly; and we still continue to receive them." She showed me also a room where the floor was quite covered with heaps of corn, saying, "I send it to be ground as we need it; but it will not last long, there are so many mouths!"

During the many days that I visited Signora Maria, I noticed several things which seemed to me different from other orphan asylums which I have seen. To be sure, I have not seen a great many; but from what little I have been able to observe, I have taken an impression that orphan girls usually have their hair cut close to their heads, and wear the very ugliest clothes that can possibly be obtained, and that their clothes are made so as to fit no one in particular. Also I think that they are apt to look dull and dispirited, with a general effect of being educated by machinery, which is not pleasant. Signora Maria's little girls, on the contrary, are made to look as pretty as is possible in the poor clothes which are the best that can be afforded for them. Their cotton handkerchiefs are of the gayest patterns, their hair is arranged becomingly, so as to make the most of the light curls of one, or the heavy braids of another; and most of them wear little gold earrings. And if one speaks to them, they answer with a pleasant smile and do not seem frightened. I do not think that the dear old lady keeps them under an iron rule, by any means. Another thing which I noticed was, that while many of the younger children, who had been but a little while in the place, looked rather sickly, and showed still the marks of poverty and neglect, the older girls, who had been there for several years, had, almost without exception, an appearance of vigorous health. It was my good fortune to be there once on washing day, when a number of girls, apparently from fifteen to twenty years old, bare-armed (and some of them bare-footed), were hanging out clothes to dry in the cortile; and such a picture of health and beauty I have seldom seen, nor such light, strong, rapid movements, nor such evident enjoyment of their work. Next to the room where I did most of my work, was a long narrow room where many of the women and elder girls used to work together. An inscription in large black letters hung on the wall, "Silentium." I suppose it must have been put there with an idea of giving an orderly, conventual air to the place; perhaps it may have served that purpose, it certainly did no other. The door was open between us, and the lively talking that went on in that room was incessant. Once, the old lady by my side called to them "Tose!" and I thought that she was calling them to order; but it proved that she only wanted to have a share in the conversation. When not sitting for her portrait, she used to sew, or knit, as she sat beside me; she could do beautiful mending, and never wore spectacles. She told me that she had worn them until a few years before, when *her sight had come back quite strong as in youth.*

But I must allow, in speaking of my friends of the orphan asylum, that some of their religious observances are a little—peculiar.

In the large garden, on the side where Signora Maria has her flower border ("We cannot afford much room for flowers," Annetta says, "but they are the delight of the Superiora!"), is a long walk under a canopy of grape-vines, leading to a niche where stands, under the thick shade, a large wooden Madonna of the Immaculate Conception. She is very ugly, and but a poor piece of carving; a stout heavy woman in impossible drapery, and with no expression whatsoever. The seven stars (somewhat rusty and blackened by the weather) are arranged on a rather too conspicuous piece of wire about her head. The last time I saw her, however, she had much improved, if not in beauty or sanctity, at least in cleanliness of appearance; which Annetta accounted for by saying, complacently, "I gave her a coat of white paint, myself; *oil* paint; so now she will look well for a long time to come, and the rain will not hurt her."

I observed that some one had placed a rose in the clumsy wooden hand, and that her ears were ornamented with little garnet earrings. Annetta said, "The girls put together a few soldi, and bought those earrings for the Madonna; they are very cheap ones: and I bored the holes in her ears myself, with a gimlet." *

Before this Madonna the girls go on summer afternoons to sing the litanies, and apparently find their devotion in no way disturbed by the idea of Annetta's tinkering. She seems to do pretty much all the

---

* There is no passage in all these histories which claims from the general reader more tender and loving attention; or in reading which he ought to repent more solemnly of light thought and scornful mood, or to remember with more shame the iconoclasm of Churches that had neither sense nor charity.

carpentering and repainting that are wanted about the establishment, and is just as well pleased to "restore" the Madonna as anything else.

I was very sorry, at last, when the time came to say good-bye to the peaceful old house and its inmates. The Superiora, on the occasion of her last sitting, presented me with a very pretty specimen of the girls' work, a small pincushion surrounded with artificial flowers, and surmounted by a dove, with spread wings, in white linen: its shape, and even feathers, quite wonderfully represented by means of the peculiar starching process which I have tried to describe. I can only hope that the dear old lady may be spared to the utmost limit of life in Bassano, which would give her many years yet; for it is sad to think of the change that must come over the little community when she is taken away. She is still the life of the house, her influence is everywhere; she reminds me always of the beautiful promise, "They shall yet bear fruit in old age.'" Once I was expressing to her my admiration for the institution, and she said, "It is a *happy* institution."

And so it is; but it is she who has made it so.

———

Pardon me, dear Francesca. She,—yes, and Annetta, and Don Giorgio, and the dead Paola, yet living "near to heaven," but with them; and the obedient souls and joyful hearts of every orphan child, recognising the Mother given her again by God. These, and the Catholic traditions of Venice; and the glory and the beauty of Lombard Italy, in her land and her people,—in the blue mountains of Bassano, and the blonde beauty with a complexion like a sweetbriar rose, and eyes as peaceful as an infant's. Think you, Francesca, you could institute such an orphanage as this between Edmonton and Ware?

But I must say one more very definite word on the question of servants, touched so timidly by Mammina. She has never read rightly either her Carlyle, or me, or —to so earnest a pilgrim mother I say it with reverent awe—her Bible... What does she imagine to be the meaning of the beautiful verses 13—17 of Deut. xv., "When thou sendest him (thy servant) out free from thee, thou shalt not let him go away empty. Thou shalt furnish him liberally out of thy flock, and out of thy floor, and out of thy winepress: of that wherewith the Lord thy God hath blessed thee shalt thou give unto him. And, if he say unto thee, I will not go away from thee, because he loveth thee and thine house; then thou shalt take an aul, and thrust it through his ear unto the door, and he shall be thy servant for ever."

Of which the eternal import is, that a good servant is no more to be turned out in his old age than a good dog is. And either in a servant or a dog, the law of their goodness is that they love their master, and serve him for love, not for bones; which is indeed the manner of every right-hearted and nobly-minded service that ever was, or is, or can be, to the world's end,— or the end of any number of worlds that are yet to be made, according to existing laws of rock, flesh, and soul.

Nominal Index to Part III.

(The names given alphabetically in this index will usually be the Christian ones simply, surnames and distinctive titles taking their chance afterwards.)

	Page
The two African children	99
Annetta	102, 106
Argentina (*the cow*)	78
Bella Rosa (*the cow*)	81
Birdie (*the canary*)	82
Bortolo Mosca	111
Catina	74
Daciana Pirani	107
Giorgio Pirani	104, 106
Marco Cremona	104
Umberto, THE KING OF ITALY	88, 89

Lilla (*with the blue eyes*) . . . 85

Maddalena Bernardi . . . 114
Maria Zanchetta (*the Superiora*) . 92
Marietta 76
Marina (*the herdgirl*) . . . 77

Paola Zanchetta 93
Paolina 75

Silvia (*of Bassano*) . . . 100

CHRIST'S FOLK

IN THE APENNINE.

BY

FRANCESCA ALEXANDER.

EDITED BY

JOHN RUSKIN, D.C.L.,
*Honorary Student of Christ Church, and Honorary Fellow of
Corpus Christi College, Oxford.*

IV.
THE NUN'S SCHOOL IN FLORENCE.

GEORGE ALLEN,
SUNNYSIDE, ORPINGTON, KENT.
1887.

Price One Shilling.

CHRIST'S FOLK

IN THE APENNINE.

REMINISCENCES
OF HER FRIENDS
AMONG THE TUSCAN PEASANTRY.

BY

FRANCESCA ALEXANDER.

EDITED BY
JOHN RUSKIN, D.C.L.,
*Honorary Student of Christ Church, and Honorary Fellow of
Corpus Christi College, Oxford.*

IV.
THE NUN'S SCHOOL IN FLORENCE.

GEORGE ALLEN,
SUNNYSIDE, ORPINGTON, KENT.
1887.

Printed by Hazell, Watson, & Viney, Ld., London and Aylesbury.

THE NUN'S SCHOOL IN FLORENCE.

I.

THE pretty stories in Francesca's latest letters come so fast, and the King's visits to Tuscany and the rebuilding of the Cathedral façade have so stirred the spirit of the people to all that she most delights in telling, that I know not how to arrange, nor where to end this number. But as in the last part there was question of what it is chiefly now vital for us to learn in England,—the right methods of schooling, or of doing without it, for the children of our own heathery Alps and grassy Apennines,—I will not let myself be drawn away from that matter; which has, indeed, been my own chief subject of thought and watching for all the years I have lived at Coniston.

We have one little school on our own side of the lake, quite perfect in its kind; a dame-school, in the dame's—Miss Yewdale's—cottage, with no schoolroom but her own comfortable kitchen, and the garden outside, into which the children can run when they are tired;—she, I think, never is. Beyond the garden, which is always bright with the first flowers of every month in the year in which flowers are born, is a bit of mossy and rocky field, falling steeply to the bed of a brook; beside which the rough path to the school-cottage winds up from the terrace road that leads to High Cross, the highest point of the hills between Coniston and Hawkshead.

And here the children learn—all that the most of them need ever know—to behave quietly, to be kind to each other, to read plain English words; to count, up to all they are ever likely to want of numbering; to sew, knit, and fit their dress in a lasting and homely manner. But when from this wayside academy they are promoted into the Government school in the village of Coniston itself, they have to learn whatever will enable them to take office with business men in towns; and sundry things besides — in grammar, and modern physical science, which enable them for *nothing;* while of the natural history of their own country, and of any simple arts practicable by peasant hands, they remain wholly ignorant.

Four years ago I tried to simplify and bring to more local accuracy their astronomical knowledge, by building a celestial globe in their playground, large enough for two or three of them, according to size, to get inside of; which, turning on its pole, might be set always to the night of the month; and the chief stars, being represented by pierced larger or smaller holes, might be visible always by daylight, and on quiet evenings, by external lamplight, be compared in their groups with the actual stars. This was done for me in all contrivance of mechanism with perfect success by Mr. Gershom Collingwood; but he got too much interested in the constellations himself ever to simplify their figures enough for distinctness to children; and we are both of us disheartened now, by the doubt whether the children of the immediate future will ever care to see the stars at all.

But this last spring, being out of conceit with my plans for endless books, I thought to write a dame-school one, on the wild flowers and useful vegetables of our own district, of which the text might be composed for me mostly by the children themselves. So with my own little farm-girl, the 'Jane Anne' of Fors 94, p. 243, I gave leave to six others, whose parents could give them plots of garden for their own, to come to Brantwood for their Saturday half-holiday; and so classed them by their seven ages to gather what they could find of wild flowers, choose what they liked best in the kitchen garden; and learn, with help of the best picture-books in Brantwood library, anything they cared to know of them. But I found that they cared to know less than I expected; and though during the half-hour's lecture, chiefly telling them how to find out things for themselves, they were always delighted to do anything they thought might be useful to *me*, I found the botanical plates had little attraction when I left the room.

But one thing I proved with success, that the Latin roots of floral names might be learned with perfect ease, forming a foundation for the good understanding of all other English words related to them: only observe, the first law of learning Latin, for children of any rank, is that they should know the melody of it, read with the full Italian vowels. I hear, with more than amazement, of disputes still in our Universities about Latin pronunciation:— of course the scholars of Italy must give final verdict ; but of all languages Latin is exactly the one in which sound has largest part of the power; and until it is sung, or spoken, Latin is only half understood. More things than this I should have proved, but Saturday half-holidays were not quite enough to do all I wanted. I must go on to Francesca's account of Catholic schooling for poorer children.

"I began this letter yesterday, and was interrupted by the arrival of my sitter, a pretty and pleasant Dominican nun, who comes to me as a great favour, that I may study her dress for Santa Caterina. She belongs to a little sisterhood here, devoted to the care of the sick, and the teaching of poor children; and she herself teaches a school of fifty little girls in the old Ghetto—the poorest of the poor. She and one other sister teach them, first of all, their prayers; and then, reading, writing, sewing, and knitting; and they also make soup for their dinner. The children are expected to bring bread for themselves, but often some of them are so poor that they come without, and then the sisters buy it for them, if they can afford it. Some day I am going to see the school, and then I will tell you about it; meanwhile, I wish you could see my monaca! She is the gayest, lightest-hearted creature in the world, and, for a middle-aged woman, the fullest of *play* that I ever saw, (though with plenty of good sense and real piety behind it)—ready to laugh at everything or nothing; and with a confirmed belief that her life of teaching, cooking, and sewing is the most delightful and exhilarating possible. How she does love the children! How pleased she is to tell anything good about them! She says they love *her*, too, (which I think likely; I know *I* did, before she had been with me for half an hour!). 'When I was ill the other day, they all grew quiet and sober, and did not want to play in the recess; and if they see me going for water to make the soup, two or three of them always run after me and want to carry my pitcher." I call her *pretty;* and, indeed, at first sight she seemed to me absolutely lovely; yet she is only a little stout woman, with ordinary features. But she has the fresh colour of perfect health, (made more brilliant by the clean white linen about her face); her eyes are as bright as diamonds, and her smile so full of gaiety that it spreads over all the faces about her. How different she seems from the people who make a business of gaiety! I think sometimes they end by losing it altogether.

But I can never understand why the very happy people, and those who give thanks all the time, are usually the ones that we should think the least fortunate. Did I ever tell you about Persiede? (I suppose she must have been christened *Prassede*, but Persiede is what she calls herself, and what everybody else calls her). Her husband was a street-sweeper, and he was a very good man, who used to rise early, in the dark, on winter mornings, to go to church before he went to work. One very cold winter he fell ill, through exposure to the cold, and after two months he died. Persiede hurt herself by overwork in his illness, and has been herself an invalid ever since. She is old now, and feeble, and very poor, and can work little; but a kind-hearted contadino, whom she used to work for when she was strong, lets her come to him, and pack fruit for the market, and gather vine-leaves to cover it, and do such other easy work as she is still capable of, that she may not feel herself an absolute beggar. You would not call Persiede a fortunate person, would you? One day a lady gave me a dress of the nostrale flannel, woven at Prato, telling me to give it to some poor woman. Persiede came to see me about that time, thinly clad and looking half frozen, so I gave the dress to her. I remember that she thanked me in a lost, amazed sort of way, and slipped out of the room very quickly. I was alone at the time; but a little later, Edwige, coming up to my room, found poor old Persiede in a corner, on the stairs, crying in such a way as quite frightened her to see! She stopped to ask what was the matter; and, indeed, one might have thought that the poor woman had enough to cry about. But what do you think was the answer which (with difficulty, being so overcome by her feelings) she finally managed to sob out?—*"Because the Lord is too good to me!"* Did you ever hear any of the people who lead gay lives say that the Lord was *too good* to them? I never did."

II.

POLISSENA "IN VENA."

THE STORY OF THE NECKLACE GIVEN TO THE MADONNA OF THE BLACK MOUNTAIN.

I wish I had time to tell you some of the things that Polissena has been telling me: she was, as they say, "in vena" to-day; and it has been one succession of curious stories and remarks. Every subject spoken of brings in some story by way of illustration. Here is one, to show that a good deed once done should never be repented of.*

"You have heard of the Madonna of Montenero? She is a very miraculous Madonna indeed! One time a blind girl went to see her, with her mother. And the blind girl wore a very beautiful necklace about her neck; and she promised, if her sight were restored, that she would give the necklace to the Madonna. And as she knelt in the church, suddenly the light came to her eyes, and she saw as well as any one. So she hung up her necklace in the church, and came away very happy. But on the road she grew thoughtful, and when her mother said to her, Clementina, this is a great mercy that you have received!

* Does not Polissena think the story shows a little more than that?

she answered, Yes; but I am without my necklace! When suddenly she felt the necklace about her neck; and, at the same moment, the light went out from her eyes. She took the necklace back to the Madonna afterwards, but she never saw again."

III.

FRANCESCA'S BEE.

But as for my bee, one bee of the same kind looks very much like another, and I cannot say *certainly* that the same one comes back every year; only this much *is* certain, that a very large and magnificently beautiful dark-blue bee, with brilliant transparent wings, *precisely like sapphire*, (and always *apparently* the same), has come to my terrace, now, every spring for the last six or seven years, usually also making me a visit in my working room: and he is so gentle that he will let me stand close by and watch him while he gathers honey. I shall never forget my horror when a lady told me once that I ought to kill that bee, and give him to some collector. (But she meant no harm, for she did not know of our friendship.)*

Here *is* my bee, flown into the room just as I began to write! He makes himself perfectly at home, examining all the flowers, and hums about as if he were in a field, often close to my face. I wonder if he knows me! Polissena, who has kept bees, says† that they are "blessed of the Lord,' and that, whenever one goes to the hive, one should ask for a blessing in the Lord's

---

* Sorella, dear, it is far worse to do or think harm, in folly than in passion. That is one of the chief things I have had to reiterate in Fors; I will look the places up for you.

† Was this on the "in vena" day?

name. She says, if one omits this custom "the bees don't like it!"

It is certainly true that bees like to be talked to; and that they know their masters, and become attached to them; and some people whom I knew once, who undertook to keep bees on scientific principles, without making companions of them, made a miserable failure of it; but perhaps that had nothing to do with it. They are curious creatures; I don't believe we know much about them.

You will like to hear, Sorel, that mine have built, now these three years, in the roof of the Brantwood dining-room, which I built the walls of, and *planned* the roof,— but was surprised to hear afterwards from the builder that he would not like me to put flower-pots on it. Any way, the bees found it comfortable inside. They swarmed round the turret, and the servants were surprised to see me walk through the musical mist of them. But people say I have no "small talk," so I didn't try my wits at them. They found a hole in the slates somewhere,—went in,—and we have never been able to get an ounce of honey out of them since; though just before I left this last August, for St. Albans, they were in a great fuss at the edges of the slates, going out and in like ants.—J. R., *Sept.* 1887.

IV.

ENRICHETTA'S NIGHTINGALES.

Enrichetta lets no one shoot or annoy the birds about her villa at Viesca, and (as they soon find out where they are safe) a whole tribe of nightingales has taken possession there, and you can imagine what music she has. I have heard one, when I was in the shady walk in her garden, begin that long, sweet whistle of his close beside me, almost within reach of my hand; and then go on with such a song as took my breath away, not minding my presence in the least!

V.

ROSITA AND ANGELINA.

I am afraid that this letter which I am writing you to-day will not be a very lively one, for I have had a sober time since my return, having had Angelina ill again, and her husband away, and no one with her but Rosita, the pretty excitable South American niece of whom I wrote you from Bassano, and who brought such an element of gaiety into our quiet life there, that I felt myself quite lost for a while. I should as soon have thought of being taken care of in illness by a Brazilian humming-bird; but, would you believe it? that "fiamma di fuoco," as we used to call her at Bassano, turned out to be the most tender and devoted of nurses, and the most judicious, too. She never went out of the house, received no visit from any one, and refused altogether to leave her aunt for even a short time, eating and sleeping by her bedside; and seemed to know by a sort of instinct exactly what should be done for her relief. How little we know about people until we see them in trouble.

But now I want to tell you about what I call a wonderful Providence, with regard to these friends of mine, which came about, *indirectly*, through you.

Mammina was saying this morning, that everything relating to you seems to bring a blessing not only to us but to others. On the first day when Angelina was able to sit up, as I sat near her, they began to ask me about you, and your illness this summer, and I told them, among other things, about those three texts in the Bible, which I touched as if by accident. They seemed very much impressed, and I told them also about the lily, and Polissena's prophecy, and about how kind my cousin Joan was, and all the rest. The next day Angelina sent Rosita to see me: she was very pale and quiet, being quite worn out with what she had been through, in Angelina's illness. As soon as she was seated in my room, she asked me if I could let her see the book in which I found those beautiful words. There was a Testament on the table; a very pretty copy, which I had just bought to give to my little sposo Pierino. I showed it to her; she had never seen one before; and as she opened it at random, and began to read, she was utterly overpowered by the beauty of what she found. Her eyes filled with tears; she said that she had never heard anything like that, and we passed the rest of the visit in reading it together. When she went away, as I found she cared so much about it, I gave it to her, she promising to read a little every day. (If you had seen how she cried over the raising of Lazarus!) The next day, when I went to Angelina, she began to ask me, almost with the first breath, if I could not find a book like that for *her*. She was quite as much in love with it as her niece, and they had been reading it together all the evening;

and now she says that she wants to read a little every day, like Rosita. And so Mammina has just gone up there to take her one. So the comfort that was given to me in your illness has been the means of giving comfort to two other hearts that needed and that are ready to receive it; for if the Kingdom of Heaven is for those who are like little children, it must certainly be for Angelina and Rosita.

But, as usual, my story has grown too long, and I am afraid I have not told it very connectedly, for while I was writing, I have had poor Bice to see me, and one of the widows, both in much trouble, and with sad stories for me to listen to; but, thanks to you and Ida, I was able to send them away with lighter hearts than they came. Oh dear, here comes another. There seems to be no end to it to-day; 'and just when I wanted to have a quiet time, and enjoy myself writing to you.

I never told you what I wanted to about that good Signor Fontana, who made the first part of the journey with us, and now I have hardly left room. We were talking to him about a noble and rich lady of Bassano, (that is, her ancestors were noble, but I am afraid they used up all the nobility themselves, and did not leave her any,) who has occasioned a great deal of indignation among those old-fashioned people, by reducing the gains of her contadini, who were so poor, before, that the priest had to spend all his little income for them; they had no salt for their polenta, excepting what he gave them. Her excuse was that the taxes ate up so large a part of *her* gains (which was true). Fontana said that he, on the contrary, had given up the right which all padroni think they have, to take milk, eggs, fruit, and other provisions for their families from the contadini without paying for them; and he said that in consequence he gained *much more* from his land than harder masters did; as the contadini, from affection, made his interests their own, and took good care of all that belonged to him. I tell you this because it fits in so well with what you told us in the Songs, that the Italians can only be helped and guided by love. But I think he has more right to put "Nobile" before his name than *she* has, if he *did* make his fortune out of cake and sugar-plums. Her contadini are preparing to emigrate. But the paper cuts me short. Good-bye. Love from Mammina and me. Your affectionate

SORELLA.

FLORENCE, *November* 3*rd*, 1885.

VI.
INTO GOOD HANDS.

I am delighted that you liked my little account of the royal visit to Lucca, and that you think you can make use of it. One little incident, rather pretty, Edwige told me, but I do not know if it be true. There are all sorts of stories about. A contadino had come down to Lucca from somewhere in the mountains, with a petition which he wished to present to the King; but when he saw him, with his *seguito*, he did not know who he was. (Probably the poor man's only idea of a king was gathered from some picture of the Adoration of the wise men.) So he looked at all of them, and rather thought the King was not there, but perhaps one of those gentlemen would convey the paper to him. And being taken with the King's pleasant face, he went to him, in preference to any of the others, and put the paper into his hands, saying, "I will leave it with you, sir; I rather think I have given it into good hands." At which the King smiled, and said, "Yes, you have."

They have all gone now, and the feasts are over, the banners taken down, and only the sight of the Duomo to remind us what has been. I am not at all sorry to have the city quiet again; the only show I went to see was the flower show, where Letizia *would* take me, rather against my will; but I was glad I went, for some of the plants were very wonderful, especially the palm trees. (I will not say anything about the orchids, knowing your opinion of them.) The plants "developed by cultivation" I do not care quite so much about, and often think them prettier in their natural

state; but those splendid **palms** and tropical ferns I would never **be tired of** looking at.*
There was **one hall devoted** to the sale of vases † of flowers, pictures of flowers, etc., and among them some porcelain and terra cotta figures; and I bought a lovely copy of the Madonna by Donatello, in basso-rilievo, **for the** terrace,‡ and paid **for it** *eight francs!* The strange thing was **that it was almost** the only pretty thing, and nobody had **bought it;**—**and all** the *ugly* things cost a great deal more, and many of *them* were sold! There was a little figure close by my Madonna, of a very vulgar, disagreeable old man, drinking some-

---

* **Are** you ever tired of looking at the *un*splendid Arctic **ones**, then, Sorella?

† Vases? How far exalted, and by what skill, above a red flower-pot?

‡ Of **Francesca's** town garden, often elsewhere referred **to**.

thing out of a cup,—thirty francs! They told me it was because that was *original*, and that such subjects were more fashionable now than Madonnas! But it is dreadful to see the representations of *old age* that seem to be the fashion just now, with all the dignity and beauty of old age left out.*

I have been interrupted two or three times, and must now end. Only I must tell you of a rather sweeping compliment that Mammina received yesterday, for I am sure it will make you smile. I had quoted her example about something, when Edwige silenced me indignantly. "I hope, Signorina, you don't mean to compare our Signora to *other people.* She has more sense when she is asleep than they have when they are awake!"

* And all its *in*dignity put in.

We are going to Venice on Tuesday if nothing happens. The Rookes came to say good-bye yesterday. I was sorry to part from the children, who have often brightened me up this winter when I have needed it. Laddie says he is coming back when he is a man, to buy marble at Carrara, because he means to be a sculptor. But he changes professions often. The last time I saw him he had made up his mind to be an engine driver, and the time before that an admiral. Good-bye, and love from us both as ever; and that all may be well with you is the constant prayer of

Your affectionate
SORELLA.

FLORENCE, *May 26th*, 1887.

VII.
RIVALTA.

My last letter from L'Abetone was to you, and now I write to you the first word from Rezzonico. I am beginning soon, only the first day of October (1886) to-day, and we arrived in the evening, day before yesterday. Silvia has arranged for our annual pilgrimage to Castelfranco and the Giorgione Madonna, to-morrow; and on Monday Signor Bortolo is going to take *me* to Rivalta, to look up what information we can about the saintly Catina da Rivalta, the tavern keeper, of whom he says that she is the only human being for whom he ever felt a true veneration.

It was such a beautiful journey!* The rose-bushes that were such masses and

---

* From L'Abetone.

garlands of blossom when we went up the road in the spring, were all covered now with their scarlet berries, close together like strings of coral; and the fields that were then carpets of flowers, had been mown, and great flocks of sheep and lambs turned in to eat the short grass of the second growth. For the first three miles or so, the banks along the roadside were all scattered with clusters of fringed gentian, and with the splendid S. Pellegrino thistle, nearly as large as a sun-flower, pure white, and shining like mother-of-pearl, (do you know it?)* And then we came into the country of blackberries and bluebells, and so on to S. Marcello, among the chestnut trees, where we passed the night.

* Well, I'm afraid not, little Sorel; but you know, the *flavour* of thistle is all that concerns *me!* *You* can find solar phenomena in them, of course, be they no bigger than daisies.

I have lost a lovely bit of a Francesca letter, first disclaiming all power of describing or drawing Catina's country, and then gradually kindling and glittering into lights and shades on it; till, pushed to do what she can for me, by my total ignorance of anything but the blue outlines of the Alps beyond Bassano seas, like purple clouds from Venice, she begins delightfully thus:—

The road all the way from Bassano to the Sette Comuni is the most beautiful that can be imagined, especially in the higher parts, where it winds often through woods filled with the most beautiful of mountain flowers; and at nearly every turn we see the great plain spread out beneath us like the sea, widening always (in appearance) under our eyes as we ascend, sprinkled with cities and villages, and with hills rising out of it like islands. Finally, after a day's journey, about sunset, one finds oneself in another plain, (or rather a great stretch of undulating country,) very high up in the air. One of the great 'altopiani' of the Alps; the inhabitants say, *the* great altopiano, the most wonderful of all. But it is only fair to say that I saw it under unfavourable circumstances. 1882 was a year of drought, and of much suffering among the cattle; the grass was burnt and dry, the ponds were shrunken into pools with wide margins of baked clay; and the road was fine white dust that every breath set in motion. One peculiarity of the country is that you never feel as if you were among the mountains at all. The horizon on all sides is low, and not very distant; the ground forming itself everywhere into long low swells. But constantly, as one draws near the edge, the top of some faraway mountain of wild and fantastic shape rises in sight, so distant as to appear little more than a blue shadow in the sky, and makes one remember, for a moment only, the immense country between it and us, lying almost under our feet. And if one goes far enough to find a looking-off place, the precipices which divide us from the lower world are something terrible to see! There are fir woods in the country, one not more than half a mile from Asiago, where we often went; but the road to it was bare, dusty, and dismal. And Asiago itself was of unpromising appearance at first sight. It consists of one long street paved with round pebbles, and houses on each side,—but such houses! They were roofed with thatch (often black and decayed), or else with wooden shingles; and (to avoid danger from fire) there were no external chimneys! The smoke escaped through a hole in the back of the fireplace, and of course blackened all the side of the house. There was a small church dedicated to St. Sebastian, with a simple but very pretty old steeple, the only thing deserving the name of architecture in the place; and there was a large new church standing a little back from the town, not handsome, but interesting, as having been built by the people themselves under the instigation of certain missionaries who travelled through those mountains some years ago, and held what the Americans would call "revival services;" on which occasion the old church was found to be too small. The new church looked too large for the town, but was always well filled on Sunday, when troops of contadini poured in from the country around. As for the farmhouses, and little villages in the country, they were in appearance wretched beyond anything that I ever saw in Italy. A Tuscan contadino would hardly put his cattle in such hovels. And all this was the stranger, because the country, in most respects poor, was very rich in building materials, having great quantities of both red and white marble. The land seemed mostly poor, the few trees were stunted, and the fields were fenced with upright slabs of marble, set in rows and round at the top, so as to give the impression of gravestones,—a sad substitute for the Tuscan hedges. All these are first impressions. On the other hand, in the city the windows and little balconies (of wood or hammered iron) were filled with beautiful plants, especially geraniums and carnations, which blossomed out as the season advanced; and it was generally confessed, even by strangers, that there were no such carnations anywhere as those of Asiago for size and colour.

And I soon found out that Asiago put decidedly its "worst foot foremost." The houses were much better within than without, having large comfortable rooms with rather low ceilings of fir beams, and floors (if I remember rightly) of fir planks, uncarpeted and unpainted, but kept very clean, and showing the pretty grain of the wood. And most of these houses had carefully-kept gardens behind them, unseen from the street. Many of the inhabitants were wealthy people (their property consisting for the most part, like that of the patriarchs, in cattle), and nearly all were intelligent and well instructed, paying great attention to learning. You ask me what has kept them so intelligent, honest, and pious ; but these are questions that I cannot answer.

Meanwhile I have been reading a book by Signor Nalli, in which I find that our friend Catina came of a very ancient and honourable family—Benetti. For you must know that our Asiago friends are very particular about genealogies, and follow them up to remote antiquity. The tradition uniformly received among the people is that the altopiano of the Sette Comuni was settled by the Cimbri, who took refuge in that nearly inaccessible country after their defeat by the Romans under Caius Marius, in the year 104 B.C. Other tribes came there afterwards, but the people usually call themselves *Cimbri*, and a language called 'Cimbro' still exists among them, though beginning to die out. There is one priest who still preaches in it, and some devotional books have been printed in Cimbro at the printing-office of Asiago. These Cimbri had a purer faith than their conquerors, and adored one God, (probably the true one,) called in their language I E S I V (written in Cimbrian characters ו ש ה). And six families of Asiago prove the purity of their descent by Cimbrian characters on their shields, of whom one, the Benetti, bear the Divine name itself. (The contadine families have still the habit of eating from dishes marked with the name of our Lord.) All of which looks as if Catina's family were pious people, even to the most remote generation. The Benetti house stood nearly opposite to the tavern of the Golden Star, where we lodged at Asiago.

VIII.

ST. MARK STILL PREACHES.

VENICE, *July* 1887.

For myself I am glad to be here again, after a winter troubled in many ways. Every day we go to St. Marco, and I have never seen the time yet when I was ready to leave it. There never was such another church; every year when we come back it seems more beautiful than when we left it. Mammina takes the "Stones of Venice," and reads us the explanation of the mosaics, etc., which adds greatly to both our enjoyment and understanding of them. She reads it in Italian, translating as she goes along, that Signor Bortolo and Edwige may enjoy it all with us. Yesterday she was reading outside of the church; it was the passage at page 147, describing the "archivolt on the

left hand of great entrance," and we were
comparing it carefully, word by word, with
the original, when a workman in his
shirt sleeves, crossing the square, stopped
behind her and listened with the deepest
interest to it all. When he saw that he
was observed, he drew back a step, but
immediately returned and remained until the
end. There is one passage (and only one
so far as I have gone) in the book which
does not quite agree with my experience. I
mean the one in which you say that the
old mosaics have no longer any power over
people's minds. I think that simple people
still feel the power of those simple pictures;
they came from the heart, and they go to
the heart, and always will, I believe.* The

* Yes, when the head is strong enough to show
them the way. Edwige, and the little old woman
with the bright, sweet, *sensible* face, are not to be

other day Edwige and I—the others had left us—were standing near the mosaics of St. Christopher, in the atrio, when I heard an excited voice close behind us, "I wonder if you know what it means." I turned, and saw a little old woman, with a bright, sweet, sensible face, coloured like a little withered red-cheeked apple, with sparkling black eyes, and a black shawl drawn over her beautiful silver hair. And without waiting for an answer, she broke out into her explanation of the mosaic,—not much like one of yours, but very good in its way. (I thought her rather patronising towards St. Christopher, whom she kept calling "poveretto," but she used the word affectionately, and, being herself of great age, had, I thought, a certain grandmotherly feeling towards him.). And

classed wholly among 'simple' people, any more than Francesca herself.

she told the story in Venetian, with great expression, unconsciously acting it all out with her small withered hands, in the most graceful and natural manner possible. It was plain that she felt quite certain it was every word true. Edwige said (I thought with much reason) when we left the church, "I think the people who built this church must have been very wise; but the church itself is made for common people, because it is all arranged so that we can understand it. The pictures are all stories out of the Gospel, and there are no learned inscriptions, but only simple words. When our Lord says" (and she looked at the mosaic over the door) "that He is the gate, and any one who enters by Him will be saved, it needs no learning to understand what He means, the most ignorant person can take it in." (Oh dear, I wish all those who are *not* ignorant could take it in.) "And would not you be happy, Signorina, if you had painted that picture? I think the man who painted the Lord Jesus in that way had a right to be contented afterwards. I don't suppose he was, though." And with this philosophical reflection she ended for the time, but the other day she talked with me a good deal about her spiritual affairs; and I was sorry to find her troubled with certain apprehensions about her own condition, which I do not think such a good Christian ought to have. She went so far as to say that she would rather take my chance for heaven than her own! I told her that she would make a great mistake, because, as she had done a great deal more in this world than ever I had, we might hope that she would have a higher place in the other. And what *do* you think she said? You would never guess, so I must tell you. "But I have enjoyed so much more of the *pleasures of this world* than you have!" When I came to ask, I found that the "pleasures" consisted mostly in her five children. But, do you know, she always talks as if her life had been singularly happy, and says that she should like to go back and live it over again.

IX.

ENRICHETTA'S CHARITY.

I have two or three things left to say about our dear Enrichetta,—of her charity, which she kept so carefully concealed. For she always seemed to be as much ashamed of her good deeds as other people are of their bad ones; and it was only by chance, and in the course of long years of intimate friendship, that I found out what I tell you now. Nobody was fallen too low for her compassion. She would ask into her house those against whom all other doors were closed. She would visit hospitals, prisons (that is, the prisons where women are confined), she would obtain leave from the authorities to pass an hour alone with a prisoner, to see if by some means she could reach her heart with kind words, and talk of the Lord's goodness. She was exceedingly and even passionately religious; and people who were regarded by others with disgust or contempt, were, to her, only so many souls that her Lord had died for. Gentle and pitiful she was to the worst of them; always inclined to the indulgent side with others, though with herself perhaps a little over-scrupulous. She was convent educated; and her servants thought that her death was hastened by her observance of the fasts in Holy Week. Still, this was not so much a matter of conscience with her, as an affectionate clinging to the customs in which she was brought up. She gave largely in money, but always secretly. It was her maid, who lived with her for thirty years, who, after she was gone, told me of her constant, great, hidden charities. But I have said enough: of what she was as a friend, I have not the heart to speak. Her judgment was equal to her heart, and we went to her for advice about everything — in this world and the next — and have great reason to be thankful that we did so. She was a beautiful woman; tall, dark-haired, dark-eyed, fresh-coloured, with delicate regular features; but she had something so much better than beauty, that one hardly noticed it. Her face seemed all illuminated with the sweetness and goodness of her spirit; but that was not all either. I do not know how to say what I mean; but it was the face of one who lived more in heaven than on earth. She could enjoy the things of this world, too, and knew how to use them. She and her son employed much of their great fortune in buying old, ruined, worn-out estates, putting the houses and land in order, and making the contadini comfortable; and they have left everything a great deal better than they found it. She did not care for display, neither would her religion permit it; but everything about her was handsome, simple, and the best of its kind; and for old-fashioned comfort, good order, and hospitality, her house will hardly be matched again in Florence.

Nominal Index to Part IV.

(The names given alphabetically in this index will usually be the Christian ones simply, surnames and distinctive titles taking their chance afterwards.)

	Page
Angelina	146, 147
Asiago (*Catina's country*)	158
Bice	148
Bortolo, Signor	156, 166
Edwige	154, 167, 169
Enrichetta	143, 171
Fontana, Signor	149
Letizia	152
Nalli, Signor	164
Nun (*Dominican, of Florence*)	133

Persiede	136
Polissena	138
Rivalta (*Catina's village*)	156
Rosita	144, 146
Sette Comuni, The	158
Silvia	156
Umberto, THE KING OF ITALY	151

CHRIST'S FOLK

IN THE APENNINE.

BY

FRANCESCA ALEXANDER.

EDITED BY

JOHN RUSKIN, D.C.L.,

Honorary Student of Christ Church, and Honorary Fellow of
Corpus Christi College, Oxford.

V.

"ADDIO, CARA!"

GEORGE ALLEN,
SUNNYSIDE, ORPINGTON KENT.
1887.

Price One Shilling.

CHRIST'S FOLK

IN THE APENNINE.

REMINISCENCES
OF HER FRIENDS
AMONG THE TUSCAN PEASANTRY.

BY

FRANCESCA ALEXANDER.

EDITED BY
JOHN RUSKIN, D.C.L.,
Honorary Student of Christ Church, and Honorary Fellow of Corpus Christi College, Oxford.

V.

"ADDIO, CARA!"

GEORGE ALLEN,
SUNNYSIDE, ORPINGTON, KENT.
1887.

Printed by Hazell, Watson, & Viney, Ld., London and Aylesbury.

"ADDIO, CARA!"

I.

KINDNESS OF THE WILD WEST.

THE following is a fragment of a letter of Francesca's to Joanie, while I was lately ill;—the reliquary was that given me by the Capuchin monk in Rome in 1874; see 'Fors,' Letter LVI. (Vol. V., p. 219), and contained without any doubt such minute relics as it professed to contain, of St. Francis, and some other less known saints of his time.

For the message from Illinois I am myself deeply thankful; but must try in future not to make friends anxious for me, far or near, for such time as may yet be left me, in this new world of theirs.—J. R., *October*, 1887.

Polissena came yesterday, and you may imagine my pleasure in presenting her with the beautiful reliquary, but I do not think you can imagine hers in receiving it; her face changed, and lighted up as if the sun had suddenly shone upon it. First she kissed it reverentially, holding it for a moment pressed to her lips; then she sat and looked at it for a long time, during which it was impossible to make her hear anything that was said to her. She will write her thanks herself, in a letter which she has promised to bring me on Sunday, and which I will send to you, and you to my Fratello, when the right time comes. I could not talk much with Polissena yesterday, because some American ladies came to see us, and kept me busy in different ways. One of them was from Illinois, and she is a very devout disciple of my Fratello, and wanted to see me entirely for his sake. She tells me that his influence for good in the wild west country of America is immense. When he was ill two years ago, in every little country town of Illinois (and she thought also in the other States) the feeling was so great and universal that placards were pasted on the wall twice a day telling of his condition; and when she was in Scotland last year, and he was ill again, she seemed quite scandalized that there were no placards, and she had to wait for the newspapers.

II.

ROSSINI'S RETURN TO FLORENCE.

In a following letter ("Addio, Cara!") Francesca says of Angelina that she seldom sang sad music, but usually some pure piece of melody from Mozart or Rossini. It will never be known, either from my works or my biographies, how much thought I have myself given to music, in the abstract forms of melody which correspond to the beauty of clouds and mountains. The modern musician *cannot* study them, because the rival skills of instrumentation, and the confusion of passionate acting with abstract music, have rendered it impossible to get any singers to submit to the training which would enable them to give a single passage rightly, either from Rossini or Mozart; and few readers but her poor Fratello will understand the meaning of what Francesca tells us, of her sweetest friend.—J. R., *October*, 1887.

I believe I left off my last little note of thanks, when so many people came in about the festa; for the Rossini procession passed just under our balcony, and, of course, all our friends, who had nowhere else to go, remembered us! I did not want at all to stop my writing for the sake of the celebration; but I could not leave Mammina with everybody to see to, and no one to help her; and really it was a very grand sight; and it was quite beautiful to see how the dense crowd in the Piazza made room, and stood back quietly, to let the long procession pass. Of course you will see an account of it all in the papers; but they will hardly tell of the respectful and deep feeling shown by all the people. But then it is quite wonderful how good a Florentine crowd will be, when there are no policemen about;—when there *are* any, they appear to awaken the worst feelings in the Florentine heart. They say that when the King and Queen came here last, they were particularly requested to come without guards, or escort of any kind; and were told that, if they brought any, the Florentines would consider themselves insulted.

It was very solemn and impressive to see Rossini brought back to Florence to the sound of his own music, played as I never heard it played before. For they had brought together all the best bands in Italy; and I wish you could have heard "Cujus animam;" you would never have forgotten it!

It was interesting to me to see the societies of all the "arts and professions," each with its banner,—including "sellers and loaders of charcoal," and "restaurant waiters." And I wonder if anywhere out of Italy those particular "professions" would think of turning out to honour the memory of a musician, even though he *were* Rossini. By the way, the charcoal people had a particularly gorgeous banner, blue and gold. I thought it ought to have been *black*,*— with a coat of arms in the middle, representing a smoking charcoal bed ! †

* Think better of it, Sorel.
† Why not rather a winter portable pan, or an angel bringing a coal to *comfort*, or kindle, spirit-*lips* with ?

III.

THE LOVE OF THE DUOMO.

I write to you on the great festa day. The bells have just been ringing, all over the city, in token that the Duomo is unveiled; and the work begun six hundred years ago is finished. I am writing to you alone, here in my little room. Edwige has gone off for a first sight of her beloved church; she is entirely wild, and, after the many troubles of her life, behaves as if she were not more than sixteen. I had meant to stay at home until the excitement was over, having little heart for any sort of gaiety after all that I have lost the past winter; but she, after trying every sort of argument yesterday to induce me to go and look at the decorations in the Piazza, finally said in a grieved tone, " If the Signorina did not go to look at the Duomo, she would not be a true Florentine." Which terrible threat finally sent me down there, though the streets swarming with people like a hive of bees. But it was a grand sight! It seemed as if all the towns in the neighbourhood had emptied themselves into Florence, and everybody so proud and happy, it was a pleasure to see. Even the poorest tried to dress a little better than usual, just because they were Florentines, and this was their festa (and Edwige put on her new silk handkerchief, that she never wore before, "for love of the Duomo"). Banners on all the houses, gay draperies from windows and balconies; the palaces hung out their rich silks and brocades, and the poor always managed to find a bright coloured table-cloth, or *something* to look gay. I went into the church; it was hung with thousands of candles, prepared for to-day's illumination. People were passing in and out, but there was no service going on. Many were on their knees, giving thanks, I suppose. But I will not lose time in writing what you will see in all the papers. There was much that was touching, and solemn, even a little sad. Especially so to me, the revival of the old times, *never dead in Florence*, shown by many of the shopkeepers placing over their doors the banners once belonging to their particular arts. It brought more tears than smiles, to see the grand old banner of the wool trade hanging over a pile of blankets and coarse flannel, at a shop door in Borgo S. Lorenzo. Because it was not done in a masquerading spirit, but one knew the dealer in woollens wanted to believe, and make others believe, in his relationship to the great people of the old time. And other things were altogether gay; among the rest to see the visitors from the country (some of them in the most extraordinary dresses; I saw two young girls in dresses, evidently home-made, of the red Turkey cotton generally used for linings to quilts) enjoying their very light meals in the open air, at the doors of *cafés* and restaurants, decorated with plants in full blossom. Bonciani borrowed all the best of the plants on the terrace, to make what he called a "prospettiva" at the door of the hotel. A young girl yesterday in my room made the rather singular remark, "How hard it must be for people to die while the festas are going on!" To which Edwige replied, "It does not make any difference; people have to die just the same. But there will never be such another festa for a hundred years. I suppose then there will be a *centennial,* because now people have centennials for everything; but we shall not be here to see it." She sighed at the idea that we should not see the centennial of the Duomo, then her face suddenly brightened and she said, "But perhaps they have centennials in the other world. And perhaps we shall see it if we have a good place there."

IV.

THE LOCANDA AT BASSANO.

The virginia creepers are all turning scarlet, and I think I never saw anything so beautiful as the place at this season. But we have been passing two or three sad days, for our dear Angelina has been taken ill at the locanda in Bassano, and we are all much occupied with her. The doctor says that there is nothing dangerous the matter with her, *for the present*, and that she will soon recover from this attack, and be as well as she was before, (which is not saying much: she has been but poorly for several years). But meantime it is very hard on us to have her suffer; and not to have her able to come to us, when she came to Bassano on purpose. We are with her every day, and find our trouble much lightened by her extreme cheerfulness and courage. When she was first attacked her only thought was, "Do not let Mammina know." She never complains of anything, but is always expressing her thankfulness for the kindness of those about her, especially of the hotel chambermaid, who strikes *me* as an untidy and far from pleasant-looking old woman; but Angelina assures me that she is "una creatura angelica." I believe the truth is that everybody becomes "angelica" with our Angelina: she is so sweet and good that one cannot help it. And then she thinks that all the people she comes in contact with are saints. The chambermaid is the favourite; but I am also constantly hearing of the celestial virtues of the landlord, the landlady, the waiter, and the little boy who goes errands: and she lies there quite happy in her imaginary Paradise of the little hotel chamber, perfectly helpless, but doing us all more good than a dozen people who can work. Yesterday Silvia was not well, and had a good deal all day to worry her, and when I asked her in the evening how it was that she had been so placid and contented through it all, she said, "It is Angelina's example, it does me so much good to see her." Angelina was the first person who ever *adopted* Mammina, and gave her that name, and to me she has been a true sister for a good many years now. Some day I will tell you more about her and her life in Peru, where she went with her husband at fourteen. Meanwhile I must not dwell on stories of sickness and trouble, and I hope in a few days she will be about again. Marina has just this minute sent us up such a platter of fruit gathered in that wonderful vineyard of hers,—great *branches* of vine, with heavy bunches of fruit hanging between the great leaves, and *such* pomegranates burst open on the tree. I said, as I caught sight of them, how I wished I could send you one of those pomegranates, for I never saw anything of the kind so beautiful.

The evenings have grown too cold now

for me to sit on the doorstep and tell the children stories in the afternoon, so now we sit around the table with lighted candles, and my duties have become somewhat heavier, as all the family attend, and I have to choose some story that will please everybody, from the grandmother to little Bebo. Yesterday evening, I am sorry to say, Silvia and Pierino had a quarrel as to which should have the seat next to me to hear Beauty and the Beast, (for the third or fourth time,) and I had to make peace by putting myself in the middle, after enquiring which was the oldest child of the two—a question which nobody answered. My audience consists of Marina, who, as you know, has had a strange life of trouble and romance, and heroic adventures with Austrian soldiers and spies;— of Silvia, who has had enough to sober her, one would think, besides her poor health and scientific propensities;—of the little German governess, and the two children. Besides these we have often a friend of the family who comes in to pass the evening,—a sober, poor, hard-working, elderly schoolmistress. And they are all very critical, and will not allow me to slight any part of my story, and ask me the most difficult questions. Bebo last night *would* know who kept the Beast's palace in order, and cooked the supper; and they expect me to describe minutely the dresses that Cinderella wore to the ball, on both occasions; also her sisters' dresses. Bebo often entertains us with stories of his own, showing much power of invention and a sublime disregard of impossibilities. The other day, when his brother passed the examination, he asked why *he* could not have an examination too;

(he is just six,) and his mother asked what he should be examined in; to this he replied, " Reading, writing, and telling stories."

I have just been telling one of the poor women (Bice, who sat for the Suora) that you are better, and she fairly went off into tears, and said, "I *have* been praying a great deal for him, but I rather think that could not have made much difference; it is not likely the Lord Jesus would mind anything I said! Most likely He has made him well, and sent him a blessing, because He knows he is a good Signore, and has been so kind to us all!"

V.

THE PATRIARCH OF VENICE.

I am so glad at last to find myself writing to you without being in a hurry; I am taking a rest at last, but beginning already to think that I shall not care to make it a very long one. We are here at Abetone, and finding it a great deal pleasanter than we had expected. Our friends are all very glad to see us; and the strangers have hardly begun to come, so that for the present everything seems pleasant and peaceful, almost as in the old times! I was so thankful that you sent me that note to Venice, which enabled me to take the journey with so much easier mind; and now I am trying to think of all the things that I had laid aside in my head to write you about, of which I am afraid I cannot help forgetting a good many. First of all I promised, did I not? to tell you all about the Patriarch. You cannot think what a strange visit we had; at least, it seemed so to me, for I had imagined him among all sorts of grand surroundings, in some magnificently furnished room, with servants in gorgeous liveries to wait outside of the door, and he himself very stately and imposing; and instead, I saw only one servant, a rather shabbily dressed little old man, gossiping with an old beggar woman in the hall; and when he made out what we wanted (he was quite deaf), he led us up the broad white marble stairs, into a large room, very clean, but furnished without the least regard to either elegance or comfort, or anything else, I should think, excepting economy. A haircloth sofa, a good deal worn, and half-a-dozen chairs to match, with two ordinary tables, were all that I saw; and the great room looked nearly empty. After a few minutes the Patriarch himself appeared, and met us with much kindness. He did not offer me his hand, but gave it to Signor Bortolo, who kissed it, bending on one knee. I need not describe his appearance, since you have his portrait, only he looks a little thinner and older now than when that was taken, and is somewhat bent, and I thought his face looked very tired and careworn. His manners are gentle and quiet, but not in the least stately; one could hardly imagine him a cardinal: he seems like a humble, gentle-spirited Christian, such as I have known so often among the poor,—not very different from Edwige's old mother; and wearing himself out for his Church, as she wore herself out for her children. He was very polite, and seemed to wish that our visit should be a pleasant one; and he was interested in whatever pleased us; but I noticed that the mention of a sacred name brought a new and singular light into his face (which is the principal sign, I think, by which one recognizes the "hidden servants," and recalled to me my good minister, Signor Rossetti, though in other respects the two men were so unlike each other!). When we rose to go, he accompanied us to the door, and stood holding it open for us, instead of calling a servant, as might have been expected; then he opened another door, and said, "Only see how I live!" It was a room quite as poor as the first, but with the tables and chairs quite covered with heaps of papers all lying in confusion. He sighed as he said, "All those papers must be attended to, and most of them are letters from people who have need to see me on business, and want me to appoint a time." I am afraid that he is too heavily burdened in many ways, and is perhaps one of those people who take things too much to heart. The condition of the poor in Venice seems to weigh much upon his mind; and they say that he does many things not expected of people of his rank, explaining the catechism to children, hearing the confession of obscure people, etc. He was so kind as to ask us to come and see him sometimes, when we came back to Venice; which rather surprised me, as he is so very busy; but then it proves that we have several mutual friends, and among them the dear old lady of Bassano, whom he is attached to almost as much as I am.

Now I have written such a long story about the Patriarch that I have left no room for all the other things I wanted to tell you, and that is the way it always happens! But I thought you would like to hear about him, because one does not see a living saint every day; or at least, if we do, we do not know it. Signor Bortolo says that they have a story in the Veneto that the angels come down into the Campo Santo at night with their golden censers, and burn incense at the graves of those saints whom nobody knows. And it must be a great deal pleasanter to be one of *those* saints, than like poor St. Marina. I hope she does not know how they have put her up on the altar among those dusty artificial flowers, and the priest shows her for francs!

VI.

THE ARMENIAN IDA.

Such a strange thing happened to me the other day about "Ida," and it is not much to tell; only I like to tell you everything that interests me; and this is something that has gone to my heart more than I can say. I suppose you will hardly remember Padre Alishan of the Armenian convent.* He is the oldest, I think, now, of all the frati there, and I have always looked upon him as a sort of saint; he has been our friend for a great many years. The other day I gave him a copy of "Ida." I did not suppose he would care

* You ought not to suppose any such thing of me, Sorel. I never forget my monk friends, I am too proud of having possessed their regard; nor had I ever any more valued than those of the lagoon-isle.

much about it, and only gave it to him as a compliment, and because he had given me an engraving of a page of one of their Armenian manuscripts. The next day, when I was, as it chanced, alone in the house, to my great surprise the old Padre came to make me a visit. As soon as he had sat down he said, "I am glad in one way that you are alone, for I have that to say to you that I should hardly know how to say if any one were present. I read the story of Ida yesterday, and it made me shed so many tears! I do not mind telling you, though I should be ashamed to tell any one else."* By this time the old gentleman was becoming rather unintelligible to me, as when he is excited he talks very fast, and

* I have to ask both Francesca's pardon, therefore, and her old friend's for printing this letter at all; but how else could the record have been, as the dear old Padre wished, "kept with Ida's story"?

mixes his Venetian Italian with Armenian in a most bewildering manner. When I next caught the thread of his discourse, he was saying: "I want now to return your present with another, with something that is worthy to be kept with Ida's story,— a memorial of one who was like her, who was an angel on earth as she was, and who died as she died." He unwrapped, with trembling hands, a little packet that he had brought with him, and gave me a small photograph of a beautiful Armenian girl; and as I looked at the sweet young face, I saw, to my astonishment, that she was so like Ida! Just the same age, and the same soft eyes and delicate but distinctly marked eyebrows, the same pretty oval to the face, the same mouth and chin *precisely*, the same slight graceful throat, even the dark hair turned back from the forehead as Ida used to wear it! Much moved, I told him of the strange resemblance, and he said, "She was so like her also in character! She was my brother's daughter. I never saw her, for she was born and died after I left my country, but I loved her very dearly. Regina Satinie was her name; she was named after one of the ancient queens of Armenia. And much of what you say about Ida might have been written about her. She too felt no fear in the presence of death, and before she died she would have her hair cut off, and gave a little to each of her friends; and she disposed of all her little ornaments, and whatever else she had, and left some keepsake to every one in the family, and to each of the servants. And look here!" He showed me, on the back of the picture, her name and the date of her death, which he translated from the Armenian. She had died at Constantinople on the twenty-first of January; Ida in Florence on the twenty-second! He continued: "For some time I had resolved to separate from this picture because it had become so precious to me; I love it so much. I will not keep it with me any longer; and now *you* will keep it, and you will care for her for Ida's sake." I tried to persuade him to keep the picture himself, but he only became excited and tearful and unintelligible again. As nearly as I could understand, he did not think it right for him, a frate, to love anything earthly so much. "No," he said, "you must keep it, and when you say a prayer for Ida, you will remember to say one for her,—though I hope, I *think* that she is with Jesus already! I rather think she prays more for me than I do for her!" I said, "I do not think our friends who are gone ever forget us." "No," he answered, "they remember us, they pray for us; I think they do *everything* for us, only they never speak to us; I wish sometimes they *would* speak just one word! There was an old father in our convent who died some time ago, at a great age, and he asked us all to pray for him; and he said, if we would, he would write us a letter some day, all in characters of gold. But he has never written it yet, though we have been expecting it for quite a long time;" and the old man sighed and looked disappointed, then he added: "We buried him in the sacristy of the church, because we thought he was a saint. But all that ever happened was, that I dreamed once I heard him singing the Litany, and oh, he sang it with such devotion! I never in my life heard anything like it!" By this time a very peaceful smile had come into his face, though his eyes were tearful, and he looked like one not far off from the country of his hope. But oh, Fratello, if I had had any idea that this Armenian story (with nothing in it) was going to take so long, I would not have told it,* for it has crowded out so very much that I wanted to say. .I ought to stop now.

VII.

IN THE DARK VALLEY.

Mio caro Fratello,

After a week of great trouble I sit down, tired and confused, to write to you, certain

* You would have been very unkind, Sorel, then ; it is one of the most beautiful and useful of all your stories.

that I shall write nothing worth your reading, and yet not willing that Sunday should pass without a word from me. You will know before I tell you what has happened. Our dear Angelina, who has taken the place of sister to me for twenty-five years, has left us at last; gone no doubt to the heaven promised to little children and those who are like them. And this is only the fifth day. I do not quite understand it yet, but I am beginning to. One thing I do understand already, that however long I may live I shall never see such another. She passed away very peacefully in a long sleep; thank the Lord for that! They hardly knew when she was gone. But I will not dwell on the last sad days (though there has been much sweetness in them), for you have troubles enough of your own, without bearing the burden of mine. I do not think that any one ever came near her without being the better for it, and without receiving some kindness from her. She was very beautiful; (I was always sorry Mammina sent Joanie her photograph, which, though enough like her to be better than nothing, to us who knew her, does her no justice at all: like most of those fair luminous beauties, her face would never paint* well), and she was very rich, and her husband gave her everything of the most magnificent; and she was the sweetest singer that ever I heard, and every one loved her that came near her; and she had enough to turn a dozen heads, and yet she was the most simple, unworldly creature that ever I knew. She never cared to be one of the great world, in which she

* Photograph well, I think you mean, Sorella. Could not Giorgione have painted her, think you, beneath that Madonna of yours at Castelfranco?

might have made so brilliant a figure; but lived retired, dressed simply, (she hardly ever put on the fine lace and jewels that her husband gave her; I suppose Rosita has them now), cared no more for fashion than Polissena does, and had her house full of all the forlorn people she could find—the poor and the shabby, the broken in health and spirit, the disgraced by unworthy relations; all the people that the world had turned its back upon, found a true and warm friend in Angelina.

Here is a letter from Polissena, in such *very* original spelling that I don't believe you can read it, so will translate it for you. I must explain one or two things about it. The *other present* that she speaks of is a little money which I gave her some time since in your name, because it was some of what you gave me for Ida, and I thought it was yours and not mine. *Your daughter* is Joanie. When you were ill, and Polissena used to come to me for news, I told her that there was a lady who took the place of daughter to you, and wrote me news of you every day. I do not know who has read some pages of the book* to her, but I imagine it to be the Signora Bianca, an Englishwoman married at Pian Sinatico, whom I have never seen, but who is very kind about going to read to blind Teresa. Her (Polissena's) anxiety about your health is quite sincere. She always has an affectionate feeling — almost a sense of relationship — toward those whom she has once prayed for; and in all her letters she is begging for news of you. Marina is here, as you know, but this great trouble has made her quite ill. Poor Marina! after taking the long journey on

* "The Peace."

purpose, she was not able even to see Angelina. I am with her every day, and yesterday she told me a story that interested me much, so much that I think I must write it to you, especially as it is very short.*

VIII.

"ADDIO, CARA!"

The name of my Armenian friend is Padre Leon Alishan, one of the best men in the world, and who has written some interesting books in his own language. One, "The Life of an Armenian Saint," has been translated into French, and he gave me a copy of it. But above all I care for the honour which you pay the memory of my dear Angelina. I do not remember now what I wrote you about her; but, whatever it was, I am sure

* It will find its place in another number.

that it must have been less than the truth. Now that she is gone, we remember many things which, in her lifetime, seemed so a part of herself that we hardly thought of them,—they belonged to her just like her dimples or her golden hair. A "cuor d'oro" people used to call her; and only now we begin to understand that there are not many such golden hearts left. During a long illness of her husband, it became necessary for her to take upon herself the administration of their very large estate; at which time she astonished every one by her great business capacity, never before suspected. *He* is a scientific man, for the most part immersed in profound studies; and after his recovery he was not sorry to turn over his affairs to her keeping. And I often wonder if any great property was administered in such a way before! Sometimes, when I went to her house, the floors would be covered with flasks of wine, jars of honey, fruit, chickens, geese, pheasants,—a little of everything; it was an arrival from the estate. And in a few hours all, or nearly all, would have disappeared—gone to the houses of poor or sick, or in some way needy people. She never talked about it, but I knew it, because I knew so many of those whom she helped, and they used to tell me. She never seemed to care for her great wealth, excepting to make as many people happy with it as she could; indeed, she was never happy herself unless she was making someone else so. She did not do it on principle; I don't think she ever thought much about principle, for it was so natural to her to be good: she never thought about it any more than a rose thinks about being sweet. I doubt if she knew that she *was* good, though she knew enough of all the good in every one else! I think she must have known that she was beautiful, if she ever looked in the glass; but there never was a woman so indifferent to her own beauty. And how she used to sing! Just like a nightingale! You must not think that I am talking extravagances; her singing will never be forgotten by those who once heard her. Mammina says that she never heard more than one other voice in the world that would compare with hers, and that was Alboni's. I wonder if you remember it. She was a finished musician, but never cared to display her voice any more than her beauty. The most that she cared for either, was when they served to brighten a sick-room or cheer a heavy heart. When we asked her for a song, she would begin without rising from her seat,—seldom sad music, always something with a great deal of melody, usually some song by Mozart or Rossini; but there is no use in trying to tell what it sounded like.

Well, she had her troubles, poor Angelina! She was a great sufferer for many years in health, though she was so cheerful and courageous that few ever suspected it; and then she always attached herself to all the infirm, and sick, and very aged people: and broke her heart when any of them died. And she bore everybody's troubles as well as her own; and I am glad, sometimes, to think that she is at home, and at rest. Almost the last time that I saw her, (and it was only a few days before she died,) a poor woman, a servant, had been sent to the house on an errand. Angelina asked to have her brought into the room, saying that the woman had been

ill, and she wanted to see with her own
eyes how she was. I was sitting by the
bedside, and I remember as if I saw it still,
how Angelina raised herself up, and took
the pale, tired woman's hand in hers, and
sat talking with almost sisterly interest of
her ailments, of her poverty, of her absent
family, etc. Then she ordered a meal to be
prepared for her, and would have it served
in the chamber that she might see if she ate
it, and sat up again to look and see if she
finished all. I saw her give her something
else in her hand,—I don't know what it
was,—and I still seem to hear her cheerful
"Addio, cara!" as the invalid woman went,
rested and refreshed, from the door. She
knew then that the end was close at hand;
but somehow she never made much account
of dying.

Fratello, you must excuse me if this

time my heart has run away with my pen; but your sympathy has encouraged me to write you a little of what I am so often thinking over. Good-bye for now; and love always from Mammina and

Your affectionate

SORELLA.

BASSANO VENETO,
Di 27 *September,* 1887.

NOMINAL INDEX TO PART V.

(The names given alphabetically in this index will usually be the Christian ones simply, surnames and distinctive titles taking their chance afterwards.)

	Page
Alishan, Padre Leon (*the Armenian monk*)	201, 212
Angelina	188, 208, 213
Bassano (*city of*)	188
Bebo	193
Bice	194
Bortolo Zanchetta, **Signor**	200
Capuchin Monk (*at Rome*)	177
Edwige	184, 187
Ida (*the Armenian*)	201

	Page
Marina	192, 211
Patriarch, The (*of Venice*) . . .	196
Pierino	192
Polissena	178, 210
Rossetti, Signor (*Francesca's minister*) .	198
Rossini	180
Silvia	190, 192

CHRIST'S FOLK.

IN THE APENNINE.

BY
FRANCESCA ALEXANDER.

EDITED BY
JOHN RUSKIN, D.C.L.,
Honorary Student of Christ Church, and Honorary Fellow of Corpus Christi College, Oxford.

VI.
LIETI ANDIAMO.

GEORGE ALLEN,
SUNNYSIDE, ORPINGTON, KENT.
1887.

Price One Shilling.

CHRIST'S FOLK
IN THE APENNINE.

REMINISCENCES
OF HER FRIENDS
AMONG THE TUSCAN PEASANTRY.

BY

FRANCESCA ALEXANDER.

EDITED BY
JOHN RUSKIN, D.C.L.,
Honorary Student of Christ Church, **and** *Honorary Fellow of Corpus Christi College,* **Oxford.**

VI.

LIETI ANDIAMO.

GEORGE ALLEN,
SUNNYSIDE, ORPINGTON, KENT.
1887.

Printed by Hazell, Watson, & Viney, Ld., London and Aylesbury.

LIETI ANDIAMO.

I.

THE KNITTING FOR CESIRA.

THE fields and hedges at Casciana are one garden of roses, honeysuckle, acacia, gladiolus, crimson and rose-coloured lupin, and other flowers; the wheat, just now in blossom, grows in some places so as quite to conceal the trunks of the olive trees, and the branches rise out of it like grey islands out of a level green sea; and the roses and geraniums in the little gardens of the contadini are a sight to look at! The people generally look prosperous, healthy, and happy, and the children playing barefoot about the doors are perfect pictures of blooming beauty.

The other evening, when Letizia was walking out with me, she stopped to speak to a pretty red-cheeked dark-eyed baby, just beginning to go alone, standing at the knee of an old woman, its grandmother, in the porch of a little old stone cottage, among some red geraniums. After we had passed, she told me part of a story which I afterwards heard more fully from some of the people here. The poor baby's mother died last summer in the cholera at Spezia, and the father made his escape to Casciana with his child of three months old, only to be "sequestrated" by the carabinieri, and shut up in the temporary Lazzaretto. (The country people call them *cherubinieri*, but do not appear to regard them as cherubim, by any means.) There was nothing there for the baby to eat, that it could eat, and the poor little thing seemed likely to starve.

The father's sister, Clorinda, would wait outside of the wall, and hear the baby cry without being able to go to it, until she was half distracted ; but everybody in these parts was in a state of blind and unreasoning terror, and nobody would help her. So she went to one and another with her story, and at first the "Cherubinieri" stood firm to their idea of duty, and were as hard as the stone wall itself; but at last they yielded to her continual tears and prayers,—and then what do you think they did? Took off all the poor baby's clothes and burnt them, and then *fumigated* it thoroughly, and put it into her arms in that condition, half-famished! Poor Clorinda's troubles were not over yet ; not a woman in the place would be nurse to the child, and she herself was avoided as if she had the plague ; everybody ran away from her.

But she bought a goat, which had more sense than the rest of the population; and now the child is a bright handsome little fellow as ever I saw. Clorinda is now servant in the house where we are staying, and often comes out into the garden where I work, to gather herbs for the cooking; an easy-tempered, light-hearted little woman, whom nobody would suspect of anything heroic!

But I must end this, if I expect to do any work to-day; and there is so much more I should like to tell you about this pretty old town! If you could see the market, which is held early in the morning under the plane trees; it is so pretty to see the contadine women with their piles of freshly-gathered artichokes, cabbages, etc., under the changing lights and shadows of the leaves. (I saw a woman the other day, who, after making her purchases, went into church to her devotions with an enormous cabbage in each hand; which looked odd, but I dare say she did not say her prayers any the worse for them.) Edwige is as happy as the day is long, dividing her time between country excursions, the church, and knitting with me in the garden. Yesterday she had just finished a pair of very pretty fine stockings, and I asked her who they were for; she answered, "For Cesira; her little girl will wear them for her." "But," I said, "they will be too large for little Sandrina." "Never mind," she said; "when I am away from home I like to knit stockings for all my daughters, and I always knit Cesira's pair first. Sandrina will wear them when she is older; perhaps I shall not be alive then!"

CASCIANA, *May* **26th**, 1885.

II.

THE STORY OF THE SAVINGS BANK.

I knew a poor widow who hired two or three rooms and under-let one of them to a woman poorer than herself. The lodger was not able to pay for it, and the widow needed the money for her own rent, and she said to me, with an enthusiastic fervour of charity, that set her face all in a glow, "I will not—I *cannot* turn her out! I will sell my earrings first."

But to go back to the charity cart in the cholera time.* My dear Angelina threw her fine house-linen, sheets, bed-covers, etc., into the cart by the armful, and then her own clothes, and her husband's clothes, until the

---

* The letter referring to it has not yet been printed; but see the following one of the way the cholera was met at Venice.

crowd below burst out into an Evviva! To be sure Angelina always kept a great deal of linen on hand, because, when she knew any poor women who wanted work, she used to let them come to the house and sew for her, saying that the linen would come in use some time or other; and so it did, but not usually for herself. Oh what a loss she is! and what a pity that more people will not take to being good, when one good life is such a blessing in a city. Somebody had an evviva the other day, or rather, two persons had it, a little boy of five, and his sister of four, outside Porta Romana. When the cart came by, they threw in their toy savings bank, which was afterwards found to contain four francs in copper. They are the children of good people, their mother lived in the house with Edwige's Cesira, and was very kind to her in her illness, and took her poor little girl home to take care of. An unknown friend, who heard the story, sent the children (anonymously) another savings bank, with *sixteen* francs, and a message to the effect that the Lord renders *fourfold*; but I think He means to render them a great deal more this time; for I have just left off writing to ask Edwige some questions about the children, and it seemed to be a providence, for she told me that their elder sister is very ill, supposed to be past hope. Now the Mammina knows exactly what to do for the particular kind of illness that this poor girl has, and has, with the Lord's help, cured two or three cases where the doctors could do nothing; so I ran down-stairs to her. And only see how everything works in! The first medicine wanted is a particular kind of wine, and dear Angelina, last Christmas Day, sent us a large supply of just that very wine from her estate, much better than any that one can buy (besides two other kinds), and Mammina had locked it all up, because she could not bear to see it, much less to use it. But now she has given me the first bottle for the poor girl, and we think it will bring her a blessing, and she will live. Oh! how fast I am filling up my paper; and I have not told you about a poor man who lives next door to Edwige, and who threw into the cart a whole suit of clothes down to the *shoes*. He obeyed the Gospel precept, that he who has two coats should give to him that has none, for I do not think he had more than two.

I used the first daylight this morning in a very delightful way, reading the last Præterita, which I enjoyed as I always do. I think even you hardly ever wrote anything so beautiful as that description of the country church and graveyard at sunset; which has stayed in my mind all day, no matter what I have been doing, as if I had seen some beautiful picture. Also your studies of the growing grass and leaves, which my own dear father so loved to study, and taught me to love. I have never known any one, excepting you and him, who looked at plants just in that way; he had never studied them scientifically, but was never tired of finding out new beauties and wonders in them, and regarded even the most common with deep reverence, saying that they showed so plainly the work of the Almighty hand. I remember, when I was a small child, his explaining to me the meaning and beautiful arrangement of the leaves, blossom, stalk, and roots, of a clover plant, with as reverential feeling and manner as another would have used in explaining a chapter of the Bible. And strangely enough, he saw many other things as you see them, especially pictures. He was a great believer in Carpaccio, *per esempio*, before you had ever taught people to care for him.

III.

ROSITA, AND GIACOMO BONI.

We are all feeling pretty sober here about the cholera, which we do not fear for ourselves (having been in the way of it twice before, and Mammina knows exactly what to do, and is better than a dozen doctors), but it is dreadful to hear of it creeping all about the country, and now it is within six miles of Bassano, which may the Lord preserve. Marina had been ill herself, but when she heard that there were some cases at Bessica, where the family estate is, she immediately went there (though none of her own people were as yet attacked), and is now busy nursing and doctoring. She writes to me, "They have blind faith in my care" (as well they may have!), "and I trust that by taking precautions in time the danger may soon be removed." A pleasant contrast, this, to what Signor Bortolo Zanchetta writes us of the poor contadini of Bassano, who are dying because they will not take the medicines offered them, "for fear of being poisoned"! Only think what sort of padroni they must have had, to feel so! My poor Marina is all alone in her charitable work, for Silvia and Peppino have been called to Cesena to assist an old uncle, very ill. I heard this morning that he had died; the last one left of Peppino's immediate family. I fear it will be a heavy grief to him. There have been a few suspected cases in Florence, but nothing for the last three days, so I hope our city may be spared. But they have organised the society of the Croce Rossa, to be prepared for any emergency, and one of the first to join it was Angelina's niece, Rosita, who sent in her name without telling her uncle and aunt what she was doing, for fear that they would refuse their consent. If the cholera comes, she will be spared neither labour nor danger, and it is something that goes to all our hearts to see this young, beautiful woman, only twenty-five, and the mother of two little children, thus taking her life in her hand for people who do not belong to her. When Angelina spoke to her of the danger, she said: "I am not afraid; it is as much my business as any-one's, and people should not be deserted because they are sick and poor: if I die you will take care of the children; or if you do not, my father and mother will." And she said to me, when I spoke to her apart, "When we have a *call* everything is easy!"— raising her eyes to heaven as she spoke, with a look as though she heard the "call" pretty plainly. As I wrote you once before, there is just this much comfort about the terrible visitations which, for some years past, have come so often to this poor country, that they do bring out so much of the best side of human nature! Your friend Boni is in the midst of it all in Venice. He was in Germany, having finally been able to commence the journey which he had been looking forward to for years, but gave it all up that he might be of use

to the sick, and their families in Venice.
He writes me a heart-breaking account of
the poverty there, especially in the parish
where he is visiting, S. Nicolo 'dei'
Tolentini. He is employed by the municipality to distribute provisions among the
survivors in the stricken houses. But I
think I had better not write you any more
of these things, which are what our hearts
and heads are full of just now. I do not
want *yours* to be full of them. And here
is a note from Silvia, contradicting the
report of her uncle's death, for which I
am most thankful. And I have now
received your delightful letter of the fifth,
and you hardly ever wrote me a letter
that made me so happy, because I see that
you really are becoming yourself again,
and that, as I supposed, your strength
comes with the summer. I enjoyed so

much the account of your excursion down to the Waterfall, and the five children at the gate, and your tea in the country with the dog. It appears to me that I never had a meal in a country tavern in my life, that the particular dog which you describe, "gentle and modest, but extremely hungry," did not walk in to share it with me! And only to think of your being already half through "Præterita"! My only fear is now, that you will use up your strength too fast as it comes. Do pray "hold back" as much as you can! But, Fratello, I could not help being surprised to find that *you* were surprised to see how much I cared for your letters. I never thought to tell you of it, because I supposed you knew. Does not *everybody* care for your letters?— though probably not just in the way that I do. It would not be fair, though, to let it pass for the fault of the bank that the letters were not sent to Casciana when they should have been. It was all owing to a mistake in my own letter to the banker, giving directions where and how to send them. And I am sorry that you do not like my address, but what can we do about it? It would look very pretty to have the letters directed to a shepherdess or gipsy, but my friends of those denominations do not, generally, know how to read, so there would be some inconvenience about it. However, if you like, you might send the answer to *this* one directly here to the house, for I think we shall certainly be here for another week, possibly more. The weather is not very hot yet, and a dear friend, whom we have not seen for years, has come to stay for a little while in Florence, and we do not want to leave her immediately. She is Giannina Milli, the most distinguished improvisatrice in Italy, and a grand woman in every way. Did I ever tell you about her coming to meet dear old Beatrice at our house at L'Abetone?*

FIRENZE,
Di 10 *Giugno*, 1886.

IV.

THE STORY OF SANTA ROSA.

What do you think Bice's little Virginia of six years said to her the other day? She said, "Mammina, I wish you and I were just of an age, and then we should always live together, and when one of us died the other would, and we could go away together. I am so sorry you are older

* No; please tell me *all* about it directly.

than I." Her mother said, "But I cannot help it." To which the little one answered, in a very pathetic and appealing tone, "But at least do not try and be any older than Adelina." Adelina is her elder sister.

Yesterday I began this letter immediately after receiving yours, but was not able to finish it, as I had sent for little Santa Rosa to finish some parts of the picture that were not quite to my mind, and I had a busy morning trying to give the look of her silky hair and pretty little soft arms, while I told her the story of Stellante Costantina, the grand Turk's daughter, (which set Bice to crying, but then it does not take much to do that). I have finished the birds, not very satisfactorily, but as well as I could considering that they kept up an incessant hopping and dancing all the time; but I am glad I tried, for I do not think I ever

knew how pretty birds were before, and I
think if children would all try and learn
to draw birds from life there would be
no more shooting of birds in the next
generation, and we should have a whole
nation of Santa Rosas. Meanwhile, Edwige
has been telling me some interesting particulars about our little saint that I never
knew before. It seems that her mother
died when she was a child, and her father
married a woman who was not good to her.
She was very small and delicate, they say;
and her step-mother used to make her do
work that was too hard for her . . . also
the step-mother's children used to tease and
torment her in many ways, because they
were larger and stronger than she. Once her
step-mother had sent her to the spring
for water with a great earthen pitcher, larger
than she could carry easily, and one of the

The Story of Santa Rosa.

children knocked it out of her hands and broke it, for mischief, in the hope that the step-mother would beat her; but she put the pieces together and made the sign of the cross, and the pitcher was made whole again. Another time her step-mother, who had never taken the trouble to teach her to sew, gave her some linen and told her to make a shirt, threatening her with I know not what if she failed; and she (being shut up in a room alone) dropped on her knees and prayed for help; at which a beautiful lady came in, who spoke very kindly to her, and taking the linen from her hand, cut and sewed it as no linen was ever cut and sewed before. And when the little girl showed it, and told the story, every one knew that the lady who had helped her could have been no other than the Madonna. When Edwige arrived at this part of her story, Bice asked if these miracles did not touch the stepmother's heart; at which Edwige answered, with solemnity, "Did you ever hear of anything touching the heart of a stepmother? You know the proverb: The step-mother shows her teeth at the children when she gives them bread, and combs their hair the wrong way."

I have not been able to find out much more about Santa Rosa. They say that, grown to be a woman, she had a habit of speaking the truth which did not much please people; and, as she did not shrink from reproving wickedness in high places, she was disliked and much persecuted by people in authority; but those who were in trouble, or who had any sin on their conscience, used to come to her for counsel and comfort. She had great wisdom, but cared so little for her own comfort, or for the world's opinion, that many thought her crazy while she lived, and the nuns in a Franciscan convent which she wished to enter refused to admit her, being ashamed of such company. She told them that the time would come when they would be glad to have her, as came to pass after she died, when they thought it a great honour to have her buried in their convent church.

V.

THE DOGE'S DAUGHTER.

Santa Rosa is at the last touches now, and will be finished on Monday if all goes well; but I shall not send her until the end of next week,* because I want to send

---

* When sent, I serenely took possession of it, and gave it, without even asking Francesca's leave, to my child-society of "Friends to Living Creatures."

Santa Marina with her, who still has need of a little more finishing. I am almost certain that Santa Rosa will disappoint you; you probably have some such different picture of the subject in your mind.

As you sometimes speak as if you were interested in countesses,* I must tell about one who came to see me the other day, aged three years; a descendant of those doges of the Tiepolo family who did so much for Venice once upon a time, as you know. The young lady would have nothing to say to me at all, and it was in vain that I tried to tempt her with fruit or cake, or with songs or stories; she would not leave her mother's side. But her

* I forget what I said to give Francesca this impression; but I *do* like the Italian title, because young ladies may (as in this case) be countesses at three years old, but can't be marchionesses or duchesses without getting married,—which at once diminishes my interest in them.

mother wanted to see what I was drawing, and I brought in Santa Rosa; and no sooner did the child see it than she brought her little chair and placed it before me, then planted herself there, and remained absorbed in deep study of the picture. When I thought she had seen enough of it I took it away, but she made a sign with her little hand for me to bring it back, and it was long indeed before she would let it go.

I am writing badly enough to-day, but I am trying to write without looking at all, as my eyes will have quite as much work as they can do later in the day, so you must try and have patience, and I will try and not make the letter very long if I can help it.

VI.

HOW ST. PETER LOST HIS TEMPER.

I do want so much to write out for you one of the stories from Edwige's gospel, that she told me the other day, and which she fully believes.

I have made her tell it two or three times, so as to write it as nearly as possible in her own words. She was talking about a quarrel among the gondolieri, in which some had succeeded in having some of the others turned out of employment; and she said: "It seems all very sad; one ought to be willing to live and let others live. When God made the world, He said that it was a great pasture-field for all of us, and we were all to live on it. My poor mother always taught us that, but then she never did harm to any one; and indeed if people were bad to her, she always tried to do them all the good she could, because she said that was the way the Lord Jesus used to do when He was in the world. She used to tell us how one day He was walking in the country with the apostles, and they stopped at a house and asked a woman to give them something to eat. Now that woman had not a bit of bread in the house; it was baking day, and she had just made the loaves and set them to rise on a board. But she was a very good, polite woman, and she said: 'I am so sorry I have no bread, my loaves are just rising; but if you will have patience, and come in and sit down a little while, I will make a little cake for you.' So she brought an armful of sticks, and heated the oven in a hurry; and then she cut off a piece of the dough, and made a nice stiacciata (just as my mother used to do herself sometimes when we were hungry before the bread was baked, and *that* stiacciata was *so* good; and sometimes she used to scrape up all the bits of old dough that stuck to the sides of the chest, and soak them in water over night, and then work them up into little round cakes for us: they were rather sour, but we never minded.) Well, as I was saying, the woman baked her thin cake with the oven half heated, and when she went to take it out, the oven was all full of bread—just as full as it would hold! But, the day after, they went to ask for some bread of another woman, who had plenty to eat in the house, and she refused them, and said she had nothing, and drove them away with a very bad manner. And St. Peter, poor man,—well, we are all of flesh and blood, and nobody likes to have people uncivil;—he lost his patience a little, and after a while he said, 'Lord, what are you going to do to that woman?' thinking that some great judgment would come upon her; but the Lord only said, 'Di bene in meglio' (Better and better). St. Peter was not just pleased, at first, for he did not think it was quite right,"—here Edwige screwed up her face into an expression of puzzled disgust, intended to signify the state of mind of the Apostle,—" but the Lord did it to show us what we ought to do, and my mother always told us to remember it; and *she* always remembered it, and never lost her patience with any one. And she always taught us to be polite to all the beggars who came to the house, because she said we should remember that the Lord had once asked for bread, and been refused. And she said, if we had nothing to give we should say, 'May the Lord make you find it somewhere else!'"

I have been two days writing this scrawl (and I pity your eyes when you read it), and I have just as much left to say as if I had said nothing! But I must end now. I cannot tell you how anxiously I am waiting to hear something about the Capella de' Schiavoni. Love as ever from us both.

Your affectionate
SORELLA.

VENICE,
Di 13 *Guigno,* 1885.

VII.

THE STORY OF THE BISHOP OF VERONA.

Perhaps you have seen in the paper some notice of the saintly Bishop of Verona, Cardinal Canossa. They have just been celebrating his jubilee now, (but I do not know if the English papers tell about such things), and our friend the Patriarch of Venice went on to assist, and there was grand festa in all the city. Marina can remember the Cardinal's father, a survivor of the Venetian Republic. He and an uncle of Marina's husband were the last two who wore the dress of old * Venetian noblemen, which to the end they never left off—a

---

* Not older than 1700; there were no three-cornered hats in Titian's time, still less hair in queues. See the next note.

three-cornered hat, hair in a queue, sword, black silk stockings, silver shoe buckles, and—the especial mark of nobility—a white cloak lined with scarlet.* In this dress Marina can remember having seen the old gentleman, in her childhood, going about Verona in a carriage with four horses, and servants in

* It was still black in Evelyn's time, though the women's dress had then become utterly fantastic and insolent; yet still, [1645,] "the married women go in black vailes. The nobility weare the same colour, but of fine cloth lin'd wth taffeta in summer, with fur of the bellies of squirrells in ye winter, which all put on at a certaine day girt with a girdle emboss'd with silver; the vest not much different from what our Bachelors of Arts weare in Oxford, and a hood of cloth made like a sack, cast over their left shoulder, and a round cloth black cap fring'd with wool which is not so comely; they also weare their collar open to show the diamond button of the stock of their shirt. I have never seene pearle for colour and bignesse comparable to what the ladys wear, most of the noble families being very rich in jewells, especially pearles, which are always left to the son or brother who is destined to marry, which the eldest seldome do. The Doge's vest is of crimson velvet, the Procurator's, etc., of damasc, very stately."

The Story of the Bishop of Verona.

gorgeous liveries—a thin, dried-up old man, *with legs like two sticks*, as she describes him; the especial object of her childish aversion. He was terribly proud, this old Marchese Canossa, and enormously rich; and there was a picture in his palace of a dog with a bone in his mouth, and an inscription to the effect that when the dog should have finished the bone the fortunes of Casa Canossa would come to an end. There was another great family in Verona then, named Carlotti; and they had a beautiful daughter, and she and Canossa's son loved each other, but secretly, waiting for a favourable time to declare their attachment to their respective families. When it happened that old Canossa's wife died; and very soon afterwards the old gentleman went to the house of his neighbour Carlotti, and proposed to marry his daughter. Carlotti, pleased to give her to the richest man in Verona, went to his daughter and said to her, "The Marchese Canossa has made me an offer of marriage for you; will you be contented to accept him?" And the poor girl, believing it to be the *young* Marchese, answered delighted, "*Contentissima, Signor Padre!*" Her father then ordered her to dress herself and prepare to receive her fidanzato. I leave you to imagine her state of mind when she discovered her mistake! She entreated, with tears, her father to save her; but he said that his *honour* was concerned; and—will you believe it?—both he and the old Canossa insisted on her keeping her promise, made under a mistake! Through a mistaken sense of duty,* which one must

---

* The mind of the modern upper classes in city life may be broadly divided into that which has no sense of duty, and that which has a mistaken one. And the Laws of the Natural Heavens have no mercy on

respect, she yielded; and having done so, made the best wife she could to her unworthy husband, whom she survived for many years, a sad, saintly, broken-hearted woman, avoiding company as far as possible, and devoting herself to pious and charitable works. Young Canossa, to save himself and her from a position which would have been intolerable, went to Rome and entered a convent. He led a saintly life, rose high in the Church, and finally was made cardinal; and she lived to see him come back to Verona as bishop. She died nine or ten years ago, and he is very old. But it is growing dark, and I must write no more. Some day I will tell you more of Marina's

mistakes. The poor mourning Bishop could not save the cloisters of Verona from being made stables for the Austrian cavalry; the young Marchese Canossa, happy in love, would have done so—or died a knight's death.

stories. Good-bye for now. Love from Mammina and

        Your affectionate

                Sorella.

VIII.

LIETI ANDIAMO.

To-day I have principally to tell you about my minister's "going home." His name was Rossetti, and he was a cousin, I think, of that Mr. Rossetti whom you spoke about in one of your Oxford Lectures last year; and he preached in a little Italian Protestant church, composed almost entirely of very poor people, where we have been now for a great many years. He was a powerful preacher, because he always spoke from experience, and a dear good Christian man, whom everybody loved in the church. He was the one who said those words that were such a comfort to Mamma in her great affliction, and that she has quoted to me a hundred times since,—"There is no use in anyone trying to obtain consolation for himself: consolation is the gift of God, and one must pray for it, as for any other blessing." She could not remember any more of the sermon, as she was in too great distress at the time to listen much to anything, but she says that those words have always stayed by her, and been a help to her more than she can say. For some time before his death he had been poorly, but had that wonderful peacefulness which I had seen in Ida, and in some others whose time was near to go. I remember always the last time that he ever spoke to me. We were all coming out of church, when he passed near me, and seeing that he looked feeble I asked him how he was. He answered, with a bright happy smile, "Nel Signore si sta sempre bene." And then added, lifting his eyes and speaking as if to himself, "Ed il bene cresce sempre." On that last Sunday that he was with us I noticed he looked very pale, and that his step was less firm than usual; his sermon was on the words, "In my Father's house are many mansions; I go to prepare a place for you." (And it was a comfort to us, afterwards, to think that so much honour was laid upon him, that his parting words to us should have been those of our Lord to the disciples!) And he spoke as he had never spoken before in all the years that he had been with us: he spoke of our home on the other side, of the Church already assembled there and of its union with the Church on earth, as if he saw it all in a vision. We had never had the things of the other world brought home to us in such a way,—all the little congregation were in tears. As he ended his discourse, and we regained our breath, which had all gone away with listening, I could not help whispering to the woman next me what a wonderful discourse we had heard, and she and I both agreed that we had never heard him, nor anyone else, speak in that way. He read the hymn, but nobody began to sing at first: (as I said, it is a very poor little church, and we had neither organ nor choir,) so after a minute he started the tune himself, and sang the whole hymn in a clear and beautiful voice, the people joining.

The last words of the hymn were:

> "Alleluia! abbiam la grazia,
> Alleluia! il Cielo abbiamo,
> Alleluia! lieti andiamo,
> A Dio padre del Signor."

And with those words his ministration in the church ended; he rose to pray, but though his lips moved we could hear no sound; he trembled, and fell back into his seat insensible. The people pressed about him; one ran for a doctor, another brought water from the well in the cortile to bathe his forehead, thinking that he had fainted. After a few minutes he opened his eyes, and seeing his poor wife bending over him in tears, he pressed her hand and tried to speak, but we could only distinguish the words, "Gesu, Signore!" Then he seemed to fall asleep, breathed for a little while, and then was gone. They laid him in the church just where he used to stand to preach to us, until he was carried to the Campo Santo; and all that night, and the next day, his wife sat there by his side, very gentle and resigned, but wanting to see his face as long as she could. When I went back on Monday to take my last leave of him, he was lying in the same dress which he had worn when he preached, and in which he was afterwards buried, and his face had no look of death in it, but only its usual peaceful expression. The different Church members were passing in and out, shedding many tears, but quiet ones: some of them had laid flowers about him. The very little children went up close to him, and seemed as if they did not want to leave him. And so that is all; but was there ever such a grand departure?

Nominal Index to Part VI.

(The names given alphabetically in this index will usually be the Christian ones simply, surnames and distinctive titles taking their chance afterwards.)

	Page
Alexander, Mr. (*Francesca's father*)	230
Angelina	226
Boni, **Giacomo**	231, 234
Bortolo **Zanchetta**, Signor	232
Canossa, Cardinal	251
Canossa, Marchese	253
Casciana, flowers and children of,	221
Cesira	221, 227
Clorinda	223
Edwige	225, 240, 249
Giannina **Milli** (*the Improvisatrice*)	238

	Page
Letizia	222
Marina	232
Rosa, Santa	242
Rosita	231, 233
Rossetti, Signor,—his going home .	256
Sandrina (*Cesira's daughter*) . .	225
Silvia	232
Virginia (*Bice's daughter*) . . .	238

www.ingramcontent.com/pod-product-compliance
Lightning Source LLC
Chambersburg PA
CBHW031247250426
43672CB00029BA/1367